the
Generous
Life

Fedd Books
P.O. Box 341973
Austin, TX 78734

www.thefeddagency.com

Published in association with The Fedd Agency, Inc., a literary agency.

Cover Design: Christian Rafetto (www.humblebooksmedia.com)

ISBN: 9781964508016

LCCN: 2024909623

Printed in the United States of America

Contents

Acknowledgements

To my wife Becca—Wow, we have lived this journey of generosity, and you have been with me the entire way! Through my steps of faith and risk-taking and everything in between! Thank you for trusting God and for trusting me!

To my boys, Connor and Logan—Thank you for letting me use you as sermon illustrations (It was a joy to pay you $5 for each time I used you!) and also for your growing faith. You and your families are years ahead of me in your generosity adventure!

Additionally Logan, your help on this book was immense! I would not have made the deadlines without you! It's a better book because of you!

To my mom, Isabel—You and dad gave me so much in life that is way more important than money! I'm blessed beyond measure because of that!

To my assistant, Molly—Thanks for pushing the deadlines and keeping me on track! You and Logan worked as an amazing team to get this done!

To the staff and elders at River Valley Church—You made it possible for all of this to be lived out, tried, and tested. Any victories we have are shared together! We GET TO DO THIS!

What a joy! Thank you, also, to everyone that has helped with the Generosity Accelerators! We are multiplying all of this around the world!

To the entire congregation at River Valley—You listened; you obeyed, and you gave and the world is being changed because of you! You live "Blessed to be a Blessing," and it's an honor to be your lead pastor! So many churches and people will be challenged and changed because of your example!

A special thank you to all of you that have allowed us to tell your story as part of the bigger story. May God bless you for your willingness and obedience!

Introduction

I feel like I was the least likely person to write this book. As I travel all over the world helping people and churches to be generous, I think of how God used me in spite of my mistakes and gave me a platform I never thought I would have. You will read about this in the book, but I started River Valley Church on five personal Visa Gold credit cards at 21 percent interest. I gave our entire first offering away. Our church was broke in 2008 with the global financial crisis. Why would I be the one to write this book?!

When I ask myself that question, I look beyond my failures, shortcomings, and poor decisions to the lessons I have learned and the obedience I've lived in while leading River Valley Church. I had to learn not to do the math when trying to solve God-sized problems. I had to learn giving is a muscle that needs to be developed, not waiting to give your max effort once per year. I had to fight against the lie of "just in case" that holds us back from being obedient. And among so many others, realize that our God is the God of the expanding universe. He isn't divvying up pieces of pie that eventually run out; he has more than enough for each and every one of us.

Some of these lessons were easy; some of them tested me to my limits, but all of them shaped me into the pastor and leader that I am today. I may have started slow in the area of generosity, but I feel like I'm in the fast lane, ready for whatever God has next for me! I know there's more; I know that I will always have to listen and obey, and honestly, that excites me!

Now you might be thinking, "why did I buy this book?" Or "why did they give me this book? Do they know how I handle money?" Or perhaps you're one of the people that is excited for any opportunity to be more generous. Wherever you find yourself, I believe this book found you at the right time, and if you read it with a heart ready to receive, you will find that this book will jump-start a new level of joy and generosity in your life!

Feel free to laugh at me (I can handle it), but please lean into the Generous Life. It truly is a life full of meaning rather than a life full of stuff, regrets, and empty purchases. I believe all of us can live "Blessed to be a blessing" and look back on our lives someday and see the difference our generosity made in our neighborhoods and in our world.

chapter one

Lots to Learn

It didn't exactly start with a bang. We launched River Valley Church in June 1995 at a Tuesday night Bible study. Thirteen people showed up, but only four of them weren't related to me or promised a job at the church. Of the four, two of them were offended that I wasn't wearing a suit and tie (at a Bible study in a church choir room)—so offended they never came back. During the study, I said, "We're going to receive the first offering for our new church. This is a historic event." Later, when I counted it, it came to just over $300. I was thrilled. I thought, "*People are giving money to this new church. We've arrived!*"

The morning after the Bible study, my only thought was, "*We need to give this $300 away. It was given to God. It's His money. We certainly can't keep it!*"

So the very next day, I gave every penny to missionaries, and it felt amazing! When my wife, Becca, found out what I'd done, she asked, "So, Rob, just curious, is our plan to give everything away?" At the time, I had a job selling appliances, and she was an accountant. We were making enough to live on, and somehow, it hadn't quite clicked with me that this church gig would someday become my full-time job. I tried to explain to Becca that we didn't need the $300, and she told me, "You're not going to sell appliances forever." I nodded, but I had no clue what to do.

My prior church role had been as a youth pastor, so any budget for youth ministry, the students and I had to raise! It was money from car washes and bake sales for camps in the summer; I had raised so much that I boasted I could be a professional fundraiser! But handling donations to the church was different … *way different.* I'd never really made a decision about church finances, except one: At one point when I was leading the youth ministry, I was asked to attend a board meeting so they could ask me about some money we'd requested for our ministry. The meeting went on and on as they argued for three hours about a $150 expense. Three hours later, I finally told them, "I know I'm only living on a (full-time) youth pastor's salary of $16,500, but if I give the $150, can we end this board meeting?" My grasp of financial management in the church started from zero. I had a lot to learn.

After I gave away the $300 and Becca challenged me, I remembered what the Apostle Paul had written to Timothy, who, at the time, was the pastor in Ephesus. Timothy may have had a similar blockage about money because Paul painted him three clear pictures: "Soldiers don't get tied up in the affairs of civilian life, for then they cannot please the officer who enlisted them. And athletes cannot win the prize unless they follow the rules. And hardworking farmers should be the first to enjoy the fruit of their labor. Think about what I am saying. The Lord will help you understand all these things" (2 Timothy 2:4-6). Okay, Lord, help me understand. Soldiers get paid; athletes get rewards, and farmers are the first to eat what they produce. I may not be first, but I guess I'm in line somewhere. I have to figure out what my plan is and what God's plan is for financing the Church and the good we can do all over the world.

As we planned to launch River Valley Church, I knew enough to know that we needed sound equipment and nursery toys. Where would I get them? As I was reading and going through the mail, I saw an ad in a church magazine for portable church equipment. This looked like the perfect plan for starting a new church, so I called the number. I soon learned that we needed to spend about $65,000 on equipment, and I contacted Portable Church Industries to get things rolling. Apparently, we weren't the only ones just getting started because we were going to be the first customers of the company. The founder flew to meet with me, and he outlined exactly what we would need to start well. He explained that every piece of equipment would be in movable containers to make setup as easy as possible. Our launch date was a Sunday in mid-September of 1995. All we needed to do was sign the contract and raise the down payment to get started … with one critical detail. If we didn't place our order—and write the check for the down payment—by the end of July, we couldn't meet our launch deadline. *No problem,* I thought. *People are already giving money to our church; this should be easy.*

We had already received a thousand dollars from one church and several hundred dollars from another one, but the remaining people in the Bible study didn't have the resources to fund the launch. So early one morning, I went to a bank to ask them to loan us $15,000. (I don't know why I didn't ask for the full amount we needed; I guess I just wanted to be sure to cover the down payment). The loan officer looked at my application, then looked at me, then back to the application, and finally said, "You have no building. You have no people. You have no financial records we can examine. Mr. Ketterling, you're asking the bank to loan you money for an enterprise with no assets." I wanted to say, "Hey, but what about me?" but I didn't. He dropped the hammer. "I'm sorry, we can't help you."

The loan officer at the second bank drew the same conclusion, and the third, the fourth, the fifth, the sixth, and the seventh. I may not be the sharpest tool in the box, but I got the message after the seventh "No." I was discouraged, but then I realized I had an ace in the hole … or, more accurately, five credit cards in my wallet. For some strange reason, I'd been offered five Visa Gold cards, each with a $20,000 limit (on a youth pastor's salary!). We could start our church on credit. What an answer to prayer! What could possibly go wrong? (Sorry, Dave Ramsey!)

Becca didn't share my enthusiasm for this plan. After all, she is an accountant. She told me, "We're not putting everything on credit cards. I want to see at least one substantial gift, $20,000 at least, to show us that God is in it. As an accountant, that would show me this is real. Then you can use our credit cards." This seemed reasonable to me, so I agreed. In case you hadn't noticed, I'm a go-for-broke risk-taker, while Becca is on the other end of the stick. We make a good pair, as she keeps me balanced and keeps me from burning out!

On the morning of July 31, I didn't have the $20,000 gift Becca had mandated for us in order to move forward. As I prayed, I sensed the Holy Spirit tell me, "You have the money. Order the equipment." I was so excited. The FedEx truck came by … no check. The mailman came to our house: a lot of catalogs and bills but no check. I wanted to go out in the street and lie down in front of the UPS truck to be sure the driver stopped. All day … nothing.

Portable Church Industries was in Michigan. I knew they closed at 5:00 in the afternoon, so when it was 4:00 their time, I started to panic.

In the middle of it all, I kept sensing the voice of the Holy Spirit almost shouting, "You have the money! Order the equipment!" What was I going to do? I was completely convinced that God had spoken to me, but what if I was wrong? I waited until fifteen minutes before they closed. By then, the Holy Spirit's voice was so loud, "You have the money. Order the equipment!" So I stepped out in faith and made the call. When they answered, I told them, "We have the money. Start producing our equipment. We're good to go." I hung up before they could ask any hard questions and felt peace that we did in fact have the money, even though I couldn't see it.

At that moment, I felt the peace of God flood all over me, Like I had clearly done the right thing … until Becca came home from work. While preparing supper, I practiced what I would say to her. As we sat down, I told her that I'd ordered the equipment, and she shouted, "We got the money?!"

I said, "Sort of."

Her demeanor turned from excitement to suspicion. "What do you mean?"

"The Holy Spirit told me we have it and that I needed to order the equipment today."

Now, suspicion changed into anxiety. "But we don't have it, right?"

"The Lord told me we have the money, and I believe Him."

At that point, I was really glad I wasn't that piece of chicken on her plate. She stabbed it over and over like it was me on the plate instead! I didn't know what to say, so I didn't say anything. I anticipated a long, painful silence at dinner, but a few minutes later, the phone rang. I jumped to answer it and get away from the table. The business administrator of a neighboring church was calling, and he said, "Rob, I'm going on vacation tomorrow, and I got distracted during the day. Last night, our board voted to give you a $35,000, no-interest loan to start your church, and the check has been on my desk all day. Sorry I didn't call you earlier. I'll be gone in the morning, but the check will be here. Do you want to swing by to pick it up?"

I could hardly speak, but I managed a "Yeah, I will." I hung up the phone and screamed as I looked at Becca, "WE'VE GOT THE MONEY!" I started crying. I told Becca, "The Lord knew they voted last night to give us the check, and it's been on this guy's desk all day. I had to make the call to order the equipment because I had to be obedient to what the Lord told me." In other words, it's not my fault that we didn't have the money all day!

The next morning, I wrestled with God in prayer. I asked, "Why did You let it happen like that? Why couldn't the business manager have called me that morning so I wouldn't have struggled all day, Becca wouldn't have gotten angry with me, and we could have celebrated together all day?"

I sensed the Lord tell me, "You have the gift of faith. You won't have certainty about everything, but from time to time, I'll speak to you, and you need to obey. That's what you did yesterday. If you're going to build My church, you need to listen to My whispers like you did this time. You'll have to step out in faith."

This experience changed me. More than ever, I wanted to lean into God. I wasn't building *my* church; He was building *His* church, and He was gracious to use me to be a part of it. I had the amazing privilege of starting a new branch of the Church to represent Him and bring Him glory. It's not about me; it's about Him. And I learned that every dollar associated with River Valley Church is God's—I'm just His steward, tasked with managing it with wisdom and integrity and giving Him the best possible return on it.

As the year went on, we had expenses significantly beyond the $65,000 for equipment. By the end of our first year, I'd maxed out my five Visa Gold cards … to the tune of $100,000. When I share this story with pastors, I see their eyes widen as they rock back in their seats. They're astounded that I would do such a thing. But when I tell business leaders that I leveraged it all on credit cards, they smile, nod, and say, "Pastor Rob, you're one of us!" One of them told me, "You're an entrepreneur, just like me. I put my new business on my credit cards, too!" My crazy story has brought me into their world better than if I'd gotten a $100,000 gift at the beginning—although I still don't recommend credit card debt as the way to start a church! God can use even our foolishness sometimes, but we can also learn from our experiences and make better decisions in the future.

In the first couple of months after our doors opened, new people showed up every week to check us out. A couple who had attended a few times came one Sunday with their children and his widowed mother. At that point, we had 110 people. (I grew up with the church that posted attendance on the wall for all to see, but this was just in my mind! If somebody wasn't there, I knew it!) After the service, I wrote down our attendance and what it would have been if everybody had shown up. I still have those records in my Franklin-Covey Planner (and I laugh that I did that).

After the service that Sunday, three of us got together to count the money. It wasn't that we needed three people to carry so many checks and cash; it was just for accountability. That week, I saw a check from the widow. It was the first time a widow had given us money, and it freaked me out. She made so much less than anyone else in the church, and I was hit with the stewardship I was entrusted with.

That night, Becca and I had dinner with my mom and dad. Our firstborn, Connor, was just a baby. I told my parents that we received a check from a widow, and my mom immediately told me, "You can't take money from a widow! You have to give it back!"

The next morning, as I prayed, I told the Lord, "I guess I'll give the money back to her."

After a long pause, I sensed Him say very clearly, "She didn't give it to *you*. She gave it to Me to build My church! You get to steward it. And by the way, you're not blessing her. I'm blessing her." What a lesson I had to learn. This one is still with me every day as we steward His money.

When I was a youth pastor, I assumed rich people provided money for the church, and the rest were just along for the ride. I couldn't have been more wrong. Everybody—from the richest to the poorest, from those who can afford any luxury they want to those who are barely getting by—contributes to the mission of the church. Each gift is precious because it says, "Lord, I want to honor You. You've touched me, You've changed me, You've blessed me; You have all of me, and it's my honor to give this to You." The widow's gift reminded me of the Gospel story of the widow who gave two tiny coins, the only ones she had, while others were clanging the offering tins with their coins so people would notice (and be impressed with) how much they gave. Jesus told His disciples who were watching all of this, "I tell you the truth, this poor widow has given more than all the others who are making contributions. For they gave a tiny part of their surplus, but she, poor as she is, has given everything she had to live on" (Mark 12:43-44). As a youth pastor, I thought there was just a pot of money, and we got our portion of it. Now, I saw that every gift, even (or especially) from those who have little, is an act of worship. This insight transformed my view of how people give to the church.

I called my mom and told her, "I can't give the money back to the widow. She gave it to God, not to me and not to the church."

Fast forward to 2002, our church was about seven years old. We had started as a portable church, and then we rented space in a warehouse. At this point in our church's life, we could sense it was time to buy our own building. I was very excited about the future! So I scheduled a meeting in my office with a banker to begin talking about the kind of loan we'd need. He looked carefully at our financials, and then he told me, "I have some bad news. First, you don't have enough undesignated money coming in. Second, you have too much debt. And third, you have no money in your building fund."

Well, I already knew all that—especially the part about the debt. After all, I had financed the church on our *personal* credit cards. Every time we bought something, it was in my name and on my credit. I was on the hook for about $100,000 … at 21 percent interest! (Again, sorry Dave Ramsey.)

The banker could tell I was devastated, but he didn't offer any pastoral comfort. He concluded, "I hate to break it to you, but you're not going to be able to buy a building."

His words were a body blow. If we couldn't buy a building, we couldn't grow; if we couldn't grow, we'd stagnate; if we stagnated, we'd either slowly die or become irrelevant. A fearful future flashed before my eyes. I had tried to do what God had called me to do, but it looked like it was all going down the drain. It looked hopeless. We'd hit a wall. I had no answers. In about five seconds, I went from being a man filled with faith to being totally crushed, but there was no point belaboring the situation. I stood up, thanked the banker for meeting with me, and escorted him to the lobby. As we walked out, I noticed a couple who had been coming to our church for a few months. They were in the reception area waiting to talk to me, but they didn't have an appointment. As soon as the banker left the building, I realized I needed to put on a good front for the couple, so I instantly switched from the darkest depression to God's man of faith and power! I walked over to them and said, "Hey, good to see you! I was just talking to the banker about getting a loan for our new building." I was smiling on the outside, but I was dying on the inside. I asked, "How can I help you?"

The wife said, "Actually, we want to talk to you about giving a big gift to the church."

I said, "That's great. Just write the check and put it in the offering this week."

She looked a bit puzzled and, after a few seconds, said, "Okay, but it's kind of a big gift."

I went to a more private option: "Then you can give the check to our business manager so the ushers and anyone else in the congregation won't see it."

She repeated, "Okay … but it's a pretty big gift."

That was the third time she had used the term "big gift," so I was very curious. I asked, "Well … how big is it?"

She said, "We need to tithe half a million dollars."

My mind raced ahead at the possibilities, and I was now fully focused! I thought, *"Does she mean one tenth of half a million dollars? Or is the tithe half a million dollars? There's a big difference!"* Both are wonderful, but one gift changes the month, and the other changes the trajectory of the church.

The husband explained, "We've had a business deal for $5 million pending for a couple of years, and it's going through now. We want to give a tithe of $500,000 to the church."

My mouth said, "Thank you!" but my heart shouted, "*This is a miracle!*"

The woman said, "Oh, don't thank us. Tithing is obedience." We talked for a few more minutes, and they left. One week later, they made the church a ten percent owner in their deal, and the church walked away from the sale with a check for over half a million dollars.

I was in awe. This gift wiped out the Visa credit card debt; we gave $60,000 to missions, and we had $250,000 of undesignated giving for our building fund!

Don't miss this! The *problem* had been in my office while God's *miracle* was waiting in the lobby. The problem and the solution walked past each other. I think God gathered the angels and told them, "Hey, come watch this. You'll love it! Rob has no idea what I've been orchestrating behind the scenes. This answer is going to blow his mind and show him I'm more involved in his life and ministry than he can imagine!"[1] You might be thinking, does my gift really matter? It might not be $500,000, but I hope this story is an example of what God is doing behind the scenes. When we are obedient to Him, when we follow the nudges He gives us, He does things that we could never do on our own. In leading our church over the years, there have been so many stories of faithful families in the church that gave at just the right time. It's not mere coincidence; it's God's plan coming together through those who say "yes" to what he is asking us to do.

Even though we overcame our first financial obstacles, the tests weren't over … they never really are. In 2008, the country suffered a banking crisis and a devastating recession. That was bad enough, but our church's problems multiplied because our business manager had mismanaged the finances, and I discovered River Valley was deep in debt. I had to go to our people again to ask them to bail us out. Becca and I had just bought a new house, and, like many couples during this time, we'd stretched to buy as much of a house as we could possibly afford—likely more than we could afford. We thought the church finances were solid; we had no idea the situation was so bad that we might have to close our doors. Yes, it was that bad. We had budgeted a little money for our curtains and landscaping. We'd already bought the curtains and had only $3,000 for the yard that would pay for some tiny shrubs and one skinny tree for the front yard. Before buying the plants, I told Becca, "I believe the Lord is telling us to give the $3,000 to the church to help with the financial crisis." She agreed. I said, "We'll plant a little Charlie Brown tree in the front, and someday, it'll be big enough to catch the kids' kites, but it'll take some time."

We gave the money to the church, and we quickly realized our personal finances were very thin. Becca and I had very little money in retirement accounts, and we had only $1,000 in an emergency fund … we were counting on there not being any emergencies!

A couple of months later, while still crawling out of the church's financial crisis, a man came up to me after the Sunday service. He introduced himself and explained, "I know the church is in a bind. I was planning to write a check today for $500 to help, but I sensed the Lord telling me to do something else. I own a landscaping company, and the Lord told me to do the landscaping at your house. That may sound strange, but do you need any landscaping?"

I told him, "Stay right here." I hurried over to where Becca was talking with some people and asked her to come with me. We returned to the man, and I told him, "This is my wife Becca. Tell her what you just said to me."

He repeated what he'd told me about the Lord's leading that morning, and Becca started crying. I'm pretty sure that wasn't the reaction he was expecting, so I explained, "We gave the church all the money we'd budgeted for landscaping. We don't have any other money, so yeah, we really do need some help in our yard."

He said, "That's amazing. I'll do your landscaping for free."

He asked a French landscape architect to come to our house and create a professional design. A short time later, our yard had nine nice trees and beds full of beautiful shrubs and flowers. He never told us the value, but my best guess was that it would have been around $27,000! While he and his crew were putting the finishing touches on our yard, one of our neighbors came over and told him, "Wow, Rob's yard looks terrific. Would you landscape my yard, too?"

> It's not really about money. It's about cultivating an intimate, strong, vibrant walk with God so that we notice the Holy Spirit's prompts and respond to them with joyful obedience.

The man told him, "I'm sorry, but I don't usually work in this neighborhood. I only work in more upscale areas of town." Thanks … and ouch. But what a miracle God had provided!

Are you starting to see it? The Generous Life is an adventure! It's not really about money. It's about cultivating an intimate, strong, vibrant walk with God so that we notice the Holy Spirit's prompts and respond to them with joyful obedience. Sometimes, it's in response to a specific need, like the time River Valley needed to pay the rent, but other times, it's the spontaneous whisper of the Spirit to give to a cause, a person, or an organization.

Our default mode is to question the Spirit, to instantly come up with excuses why that nudge couldn't be God, why we can't afford to give right now, or why we can't afford to give that much. We all want and need to protect our families. I know I do. We want to provide the best education for them, the best opportunities to get ahead in life, the most memorable life experiences. But rather than saving for yet another family trip to Disney, wouldn't it be more worthwhile to involve them in a real faith adventure of giving?

My question to people about generosity isn't "How much are you giving?" It's "Are you following the voice of God who is calling you to be His partner in the greatest adventure the world has ever known?" That adventure includes giving, but it's far more than that. The Spirit prompts us to stop to help someone whose car is stuck on the side of the road; to take a few extra minutes to listen to a child, a coworker, a neighbor, or an elderly person who needs someone to pay a little attention to them; to respond to the invitation to go on a missions trip to build an orphanage or distribute food and supplies; to share your story of faith with someone who crosses your path; or a thousand other ways. God's Spirit wants to take us by the hand and lead us into incredible experiences.

One of the main flaws in today's version of the Christian faith is that many people have this attitude: "God, I appreciate Your saving me so I can go to heaven, but I've got it from here. I don't need Your involvement. I can handle it myself."

Instead of focusing on our limited, self-focused agenda, we need to look up and begin to grasp the magnitude of God's earth-changing agenda. We aren't saved to sit, soak, and sour; we're saved to be partners with Him in His mission. He doesn't need our money. He "owns the cattle on a thousand hills," and He's the Creator and King of the entire universe (Psalm 50:10). He is incredibly generous to us—first, in the sacrifice of

Christ to die the death we should have died, and then to invite us to join Him in changing the world. I've heard people say, "I work hard for my money, and it's mine to do with whatever I want." I want to ask, "Who gave you the talents, education, training, and skills to earn a living? Who gives you air to breathe and a heart that keeps beating? And besides, what if you'd been born as a serf in the Middle Ages in Central Europe? You'd do whatever your parents and grandparents had done for generations. You wouldn't have anything like the options you have today. Everything you are and everything you have are gifts from God. When you realize how generous God has been to you, every gift to Him is only a response of gratitude."

God has orchestrated the universe, our world, and our place in history to reveal His generosity. People a lot smarter than me talk about the anthropic principle, which is that there are about 30 specific factors necessary for life on earth, and if any one of them was altered in the slightest, life wouldn't exist. So, God is both creative and detailed. We have seasons, fertile soil, weather systems to give us rain, and crops that feed billions. And today, we have advances in medicine and science that would astound experts only a generation earlier. The point is that each of us is already the beneficiary of a wealth of blessings from the gracious, wise, and powerful hand of God.

Generosity must be learned, and it's our job as parents to model and teach it. When our two sons, Connor and Logan, were little, Becca and I celebrated when they shared their toys. When one shared his cookie with his brother, I was more excited than the brother who got the second half. They watched Becca and me, and they heard us talk and pray about blessing others, so when one of them said, "Mom, Dad, I want to help that kid who doesn't have as much as we do," I wanted to dance and shout for joy. As their dad, I cheered every time they wanted to give to God or anyone else. I believe God has the same perspective, but even more: He cheers us every time we respond to the nudge of the Spirit to give generously. He's saying, "Yes! That's what I do. That looks like Me!"

We could look at dozens of passages in the Bible (and we will in the chapters of this book), but one stands out to me. In the Apostle Paul's circular letter to several churches in modern Turkey, he explains very clearly that our choices each day and our stewardship of what God has put in our hands are motivated not by guilt or pressure but by wonder. He wrote, "Imitate God, therefore, in everything you do, because you are his dear children. Live a life filled with love, following the example of Christ. He loved us and offered himself as a sacrifice for us, a pleasing aroma to God" (Ephesians 5:1-2). Our love for God is a response to His limitless love for us. Our generosity to Him and His cause is a response to His overwhelming generosity to us. He gave first, before we even knew Him. And He keeps giving to show His affection for us. So why do we give? Not guilt. Not manipulation. Not pressure. Just an overflowing heart of thankfulness.

Just a note to clarify an important point: Throughout this book, I and some of the people whose stories are included mention God "speaking" to us. That term makes some people feel uncomfortable, so let me explain. In the preface to John's Gospel, he says that Jesus is "the Word"—it's His nature to communicate with us. How does He do that? God uses a variety of methods, including dreams, visions, a burning bush, a donkey, and the visitation of angels, but most often, He speaks through the Scriptures and the impressions of the Holy Spirit, which are never in conflict with one another. By far, the most important and most common way God leads us is by illuminating the truths in the Bible, giving us wisdom, assurance, and direction. But the Spirit often "whispers" and sometimes "shouts" to get our attention. In Luke's account of the early church, we find Paul, Silas, and Timothy trying to figure out where God wanted them to go and preach, but as they made plans, the Spirit intervened to let them know their plans weren't His: " Next Paul and Silas traveled through the area of Phrygia and Galatia, because the Holy Spirit had prevented them from preaching the word in the province of Asia at that time. Then coming to the borders of Mysia, they headed north for the province of Bithynia, but again the Spirit of Jesus did not allow them to go there. So instead, they went on through Mysia to the seaport of Troas" (Acts 16:6-8). I'm sure they were confused—didn't God want people in those places to hear about Jesus? —but that night, Paul had a vision of a man from Macedonia who pleaded with him to travel there. "So we decided to leave for Macedonia at once, having concluded that God was calling us to preach the Good News there" (v. 10). In each of the many ways God communicates with us, we can say He speaks to us. It's seldom, if ever, in an audible voice, but He makes His heart, His purposes, and His direction known to us. It is up to us to seek and listen.

I hope you'll join me on this adventure of generosity. I'll tell you, it's a thrill. I never know what the Holy Spirit will put on my heart, but I know that each time, I'll be amazed at how He leads and how He multiplies the impact of my giving. Instead of looking at what's in our hands and concluding that our impact is limited, He calls us to live a life of faith, looking at the wealth in His hands and trusting Him to steer us toward greater joy through greater generosity. So, I hope you'll ask yourself: *God is fabulously wealthy, wise, and powerful. What does He want to do with all that He's given to me?*

At the end of this book, you'll find some questions designed to stimulate your thinking on each chapter, prod your prayers, and give direction to small group discussions. This isn't a speed drill, so don't rush through them. Prayerfully consider each question, and trust God to give you His wisdom and the courage to follow Him.

chapter two

Not a Pie

One of the most important principles I've learned about money is that God doesn't serve blessings to us like we serve slices of pie. My dad's career showed me this insight. He worked for Key Cadillac as a service advisor. Like most of the workers there, he was in the union. Each time the union contract was up for renewal, I could feel the tension in my dad and his friends who worked alongside him. The struggle was always between the union and management: how would they divide the revenues? Of course, each side had a vested financial interest in the outcome, which was never pretty. I overheard conversations like this:

"Will they come to a good compromise? If they don't, the union might strike."

"Will we see Dad in the picket line on television?"

"Will the company hire replacement workers (called scabs)? If so, will it offer them permanent jobs?"

"If there's a strike, how long will the union pay the employees? Not long!"

"When the money runs out, what happens to our family?"

Each side wanted a bigger slice of a finite revenue pie, and they fought hard to get it. I remember times when Dad walked the picket line during a strike, and we prayed every night that the strike would end soon, with the union getting all they wanted. Union negotiations happened regularly. They were part of our family's rhythm.

Throughout those years, I assumed that's how we relate to God. Subconsciously, I believed I was in competition with every other Christian, and I had to prove to God that I deserved a bigger piece of the pie—that is, more blessings. I didn't want the leftover piece, and I sure didn't want the crumbs after everybody else had eaten. I wanted a nice, big slice! It was a zero-sum game: if you win, I lose; if I win, you lose. There's only a limited amount of wealth, and no more is being created … or so I believed.

One day in the early years of River Valley Church, I was upset with God because I'd heard that another pastor had received a huge financial blessing. I wanted to shout, "Are you kidding me? Why him, God? Why not me? What did I do wrong that You didn't bless me like that?" I concluded that I needed to present my case more powerfully to God. In other words, I needed a better union rep!

(In case you can't tell, I'm cut from the same bolt of cloth as everyone else. I wrestle with doubt, fear, jealousy, and all the rest.) The next morning as I spent time in prayer, I continued to pour out my frustration. I sensed God say, "You seem to have a tinge of envy."

"Yeah!" I wanted to shout. "Why would You do that for him … but not me?"

God lovingly corrected me: "I didn't give him *your* blessing. I gave him *his* blessing. I have blessings for you. No one is taking your blessings from you. You have no reason to be envious. You're not in a competition with anyone. I'm not slicing the pie. I have unlimited resources."

I thought of the 37 chapters of Job where he asked questions of God because his circumstances were exceptionally painful, and his friends blamed him for his trouble. Then God spoke. He didn't exactly answer Job's specific question about why He had allowed all the suffering, but instead, He gave Job a far wider lens on himself:

> "Who is this that questions my wisdom
> with such ignorant words?
> Brace yourself like a man,
> because I have some questions for you,
> and you must answer them.
>
> Where were you when I laid the foundations
> of the earth?
> Tell me, if you know so much.
> Who determined its dimensions
> and stretched out the surveying line?
> What supports its foundations,
> and who laid its cornerstone
> as the morning stars sang together
> and all the angels shouted for joy?"
> (Job 38:2-7)

Actually, this is just the preface to the longest speech by God in the Bible. It was all designed to overwhelm Job with the vastness and intricacies of nature, to show that God is infinitely powerful, creative, and wise. That was enough for Job. When God finished speaking, Job replied,

"I was talking about things I knew nothing about,
things far too wonderful for me …
I had only heard about you before,
    but now I have seen you with my own eyes.
I take back everything I said,
    and I sit in dust and ashes to show my
repentance." (42:2, 5-6)

My mind raced through the Scriptures. In that moment, it was like God was saying, "I'm the God who placed a ram in the bushes for Abraham. I'm the God who sent ten signs to convince Pharaoh to let My people go. I'm the God who parted the Red Sea to save them from Pharaoh's army. I'm the God who caused manna and quail to fall from heaven to feed My people. I'm the God who told Peter to go fishing and find two coins in a fish's mouth to pay taxes. I'm the God who brought Lazarus back from the grave. Is anything too difficult for Me?"

The Lord reminded me of an article I'd read not long before. It was about the astounding size of the universe, but more than that, it's continuing to expand. The Hubble telescope revolutionized astronomy, and the Webb telescope is far more powerful. In recent years, scientists have been amazed that the universe is expanding much faster than they previously thought. In fact, the observable universe of galaxies, stars, and planets doesn't account for the speed of expansion (which astronomers call "inflation"). They had to come up with the novel idea that physical matter accounts for only about five percent of the universe; dark energy and dark matter are all the rest. This means that 95 percent of the universe is yet to be explained! Dark energy and dark matter must be the reason (astronomers assume) the universe is expanding so quickly. And we need to realize God is far bigger *than all of that*: He "has measured off the heavens with his fingers" (Isaiah 40:12).

When Abraham was discouraged that God hadn't come through on His promise to give him a son (much less make from him "a great nation"), he came up with Plan B: to make his servant Eliezer his heir. God again used the vast expanse of the Heavens to demonstrate His infinite ability to bless. He told Abraham, "'No, your servant will not be your heir, for you will have a son of your own who will be your heir.' Then the Lord took Abram outside and said to him, 'Look up into the sky and count the stars if you can. That's how many descendants you will have!'" (Genesis 15:4-5)

As I thought of these moments in the Scriptures, I could almost hear God repeat: "I'm not slicing pieces of pie that you need to fight over. I'm the God of infinite resources and wisdom. I'm not stingy. I'm the God of the expanding universe, and I'm willing and able to bless abundantly." At the end of one of Paul's prayers in his letter to the Ephesians, he captures this idea that God is limitless in His love and His blessings: "Now all glory to God, who is able, through his mighty power at work within us, to accomplish infinitely more than we might ask or think. Glory to him in the church and in Christ Jesus through all generations forever and ever! Amen" (Ephesians 3:20-21).

> When we live for a bigger piece of pie, we're thinking, "How will God bless me more than that guy?" But when our view of Him expands, our thinking changes to: "I'm living too small. It's not about the blessings God has for me. It's about what God wants to do through me for His glory."

When we live for a bigger piece of pie, we're thinking, *"How will God bless me more than that guy?"* But when our view of Him expands, our thinking changes to: *I'm living too small. It's not about the blessings*

God has for me. It's about what God wants to do through me for His glory. Before Copernicus and Galileo, everyone assumed the sun revolved around the earth, but those early astronomers showed that the earth revolves around the sun. I had been living pre-Copernicus and Galileo, putting myself in the center of my universe, but suddenly, God corrected my astronomy: He's the center, and I'm revolving around Him!

Before, I wanted to be blessed as a sign that God loves me, but now I want to be blessed for a very different reason: to be a blessing to others. I now live by the saying: "God brings it to you to bless people through you." He's the center; He's the reason, the Alpha and the Omega—He's the beginning as the source and the ending as the impact.

Sometimes, people ask me if I'm a pessimist, who sees the glass as half empty, or an optimist, who sees the glass as half full. I tell them I'm more than an optimist: I see the glass as half full, but it comes with free refills! When Charles Spurgeon, the great English preacher of the nineteenth century, taught Psalm 23, he said, "Will not your cup run over now? What cup can hold your God?"[2] Amen!

This new perspective on the magnitude of God and His creation prompted me to go on the adventure of generosity. I had been preoccupied with what God was giving (and more to the point, not giving) me, but now I saw myself as a channel for God to pour His blessings through. And it's not only about money. We can also give joy, comfort, time, attention, and kindness, to name a few of the many gifts. Solomon knew this principle. He wrote, "The world of the generous gets larger and larger; the world of the stingy gets smaller and smaller. The one who blesses others is abundantly blessed; those who help others are helped" (Proverbs 11:24-25 MSG).

It's easy to have a very limited grasp of God's heart and His blessings. Sometimes I hear people complain that they gave, but God didn't bless them the way they expected. They had a transactional view of giving—mechanical, immediate, and always in kind. I believe there are three guaranteed blessings when we give, and some that usually happen but maybe in unexpected ways. The first guarantee is the smile of God, His delight in our obedience to tithe and our joyful generosity. We're becoming a little more like Him, and He loves that!

The second guarantee is that God uses our money, stewarded by church leaders, to reach the lost and care for those in need—and we have the joy of seeing the impact of our gifts. What a thrill! But can we always expect God to give us ten times more than what we've given? Some people believe that (because they've heard pastors teach it), and they're deeply disappointed when the mechanics don't work that way. Yes, time and time again, I've seen God bless generous people financially so they can give more, but we love and serve a personal God, not a machine.

The third promise is that God will take care of you and supply all your needs from His riches in glory. Tithing is a test at first, and each step above the tithe is another test. God tests us to deepen our devotion to Him—a devotion that (gradually or quickly) becomes much deeper than our devotion to money.

When our boys, Connor and Logan, were younger, Becca and I loved to do special things for them, but when they asked for things, we sometimes said, "No, not now" for their own good. At the time, they may not have seen our response as loving, but now that they're older and wiser, they understand that testing is a vital part of growing. As you give, focus on these three guaranteed blessings, and give with sheer delight. God will take care of you financially, too, but maybe not in the way or the timing you expected. If you see Him as a loving, wise Father, that's a perfect place to start.

When we tap into God's generosity of pouring out love, forgiveness, acceptance, and tangible blessings into our lives, we no longer see Him as a celestial vending machine. Rather, we see Him as our loving, wise Father. And when we respond with gratitude and generosity, our loving, wise Father blesses us and takes care of us in countless ways. When Paul met with the elders from the church in Ephesus, he gave them some final instructions because he wasn't going to see them again. He reminded them of his tenacious care for them, and he left them with a promise Jesus had given him: "And I have been a constant example of how you can help those in need by working hard. You should remember the words of the Lord Jesus: 'It is more blessed to give than to receive'" (Acts 20:35).

Becca and I know that promise is true. We've followed the pattern described in this book of Plan-Vision-Dream, and God's blessings have overwhelmed us. It took fifty-five years for me to give what I'd always dreamed to give someday. When we got there, we set a new dream goal, and I wondered, "God, will You let us get there in five years ... or maybe just two?"

> **When we consider blessings, we're not waiting for God to make the first move. He's already made it!**

When we consider blessings, we're not waiting for God to make the first move. He's already made it! Paul explained to the Christians in Rome, "When we were utterly helpless, Christ came at just the right time and died for us sinners." He then says that occasionally, someone might die to save a person who is "especially good," but we don't qualify. "But God showed his great love for us by sending Christ to die for us while we were still sinners" (Romans 5:7-8). We didn't convince God that our goodness is worthy of His love. We didn't impress Him in the least. If we made the first move, it was in the wrong direction! God poured out the greatest blessing mankind has ever known (and ever will know) when we had nothing to bargain with. Our hands were completely empty, and He filled them with His overwhelming and overflowing grace.

When I hear people grumble about giving and use the words, "I have to," I know their hearts haven't been touched by God, no matter how much they give. When the love of God engulfs our hearts, we say, "I want to give," and in fact, "I can't wait to give!" Someone once asked Charles Spurgeon, "How do you know if you're a cheerful giver?" He responded, "One thing I know, that a cheerful giver always wishes he could give ten times as much."[3]

Gratitude, it seems to me, is a sure sign that we're at least beginning to appreciate God's generosity to us. When I was a young, strong, healthy man, I didn't think twice about my health. I took it for granted. But now that I'm getting older, and especially since my heart attack (in 2014, I had a heart attack and needed three stents, but I'm doing great now!), I thank God every day for my health, the air I breathe, and even for the gravity that keeps me firmly planted on the earth. I've read accounts of prisoners of war who were suddenly released, and they were so thankful they could hardly take it all in. They wandered around for days getting reacquainted with freedom. Through Christ, we've been set free, and I hope we never get over it.

Let's go back to the beginning: God created Earth to be a beautiful place, and He put the first couple in a bountiful garden. It didn't take long, though, for things to turn south. Adam and Eve were banished from the garden, and sin has affected us since then. The next several chapters in Genesis are one disaster after another. Things looked hopeless, but God chose a man to put things back on the rails and at least begin to reorder the world the way God intended:

> The LORD had said to Abram, "Leave your native country, your relatives, and your father's family, and go to the land that I will show you. I will make you into a great nation. I will bless you and make you famous, and you will be a blessing to others. I will bless those who bless you and curse those who treat you with contempt. All the families on Earth will be blessed through you." (Genesis 12:1-3)

God's plan was never for His blessings to flow into a dead-end pond. They were always meant to be passed on and paid forward into the lives of others. This promise didn't end with the patriarchs Abraham, Isaac, and Jacob, and it didn't end when the children of Israel entered the Promised Land. In fact, the promise still operates today. The single most important concept of a generous life is that we're blessed to be a blessing. You've probably heard it before, and you're going to read it many more times in the pages of this book. It's the inescapable law of the harvest, the half-full glass with unlimited refills for Abraham and every other believer, including you and me. What a joy that we get to live blessed so we can be a blessing!

When we're conduits of God's blessings into the lives of others, we're following the Old Testament concept of righteousness. The Hebrew word is *Tzedakah*, which means "an ethical obligation of spontaneous act of goodwill or generosity; unlike philanthropy, it is a religious obligation to perform offerings from the rich to the poor."[4] The word occurs 157 times in Proverbs. Old Testament scholar Bruce Waltke points to Proverbs 29:7 as the clear dividing line between righteousness and wickedness:

"The righteous care about justice for the poor, but the wicked have no such concern."

I want to live a righteous life—not just with integrity, which is one side of righteousness, but with a heart overflowing with compassion for those in need. In fact, that's how I was designed to live. The gospel includes this concept. We often think of justification as the forgiveness of sins. It is, but that's only half of it: Christ died in our place to pay for our sins, so His death is imputed to us (which means it is credited to our account), but His righteous life is also imputed to us (credited to us, too), so when the Father looks at us, He sees us as righteous as Jesus. Paul described "the great swap" this way: "God made [Christ] who had no sin to be sin for us, so that in him we might become the righteousness of God" (2 Corinthians 5:21 NIV).

> The single most important concept of a generous life is that we're blessed to be a blessing.

It's astounding, isn't it? But it's true. Stay with me and re-read this if you have to! There are, then, two kinds of righteousness: positional righteousness, which is complete the moment we trust in Christ, and experiential righteousness, which is our increasing Christlikeness. Sanctification is the process of gradually changing from the inside out so our attitudes, words, and behavior look more like Jesus. What does it mean to look more like Jesus? Among other things, it certainly means to be radically compassionate and generous.

After the horror of the Holocaust during World War II, the nation of Israel wanted to honor non-Jews who took great risks to save the lives of Jews in Europe, people like Oscar Schindler, whose tireless efforts were depicted in the movie *Schindler's List*. The honor given to those who gave themselves to save Jews is called "The Righteous among the

Nations." Yad Vashem, the World Holocaust Remembrance Center, explains, "Rescue took many forms and the Righteous came from different nations, religions, and walks of life. What they had in common was that they protected their Jewish neighbors at a time when hostility and indifference prevailed."[5]

Too often, we have a stiff, stale, solemn concept of righteousness. We think it refers primarily to what we don't do and what we condemn others for doing. The religious leaders of Jesus's day had that kind of righteousness, but Jesus told the crowd listening to the Sermon on the Mount, "Unless your righteousness surpasses that of the Pharisees and the teaches of the law, you will certainly not enter the Kingdom of Heaven" (Matthew 5:20 NIV). When the crowd heard this, I can imagine they would have been utterly stunned. After all, the Pharisees didn't just follow all 613 laws of Moses—they added a lot more to the list! But they missed the point. Righteousness certainly includes a commitment to moral virtue, but it's more … *a lot more.* It includes genuine love for all people, self-sacrifice, kindness beyond the norm, and joyful generosity, especially to those who can't repay us. This is the kind of righteousness Jesus demonstrated.

It's fascinating that sometimes in the Bible, two words can make all the difference. When Paul explains the gospel of grace in Ephesians, he paints the bleakest of pictures about us being helpless and hopeless in our sins, yet then he turns the page by writing, "But God …" And he describes the wonder of God's grace. In a similar way, in his second letter to the Corinthians, he encourages them to give for famine relief in Palestine, and he uses two words to turn the page again:

> Now he who supplies seed to the sower and
> bread for food will also supply and increase

> your store of seed and will enlarge the harvest
> of your righteousness. You will be enriched
> in every way *so that* you can be generous on
> every occasion, and through us your gener-
> osity will result in thanksgiving to God.
> (2 Corinthians 9:10-11 NIV, emphasis added)

Did you see it? "So that." Why does God enrich us? *So that* we can be generous. When? On every occasion. And the result? Everybody is more grateful to God for the supply of resources, the heart to give, and the impact on those in need. Blessed to be a blessing.

Christians often live with a "mentality of scarcity." They believe there's a finite pie, and their slice isn't big enough. In many ways, that's just plain wrong. Anyone who makes $38,000 a year is in the top one percent of wealth in the world. Those who complain that they're poor have their eyes on the wrong end of the continuum. They look at those in the top one-tenth of one percent, so they feel impoverished. Their house *only* has two bathrooms; they *only* have three televisions; they can *only* afford two $25,000 cars, and they can *only* take two vacations a year. If they looked in the other direction, they'd realize they're fabulously wealthy because God has already abundantly blessed them! Instead of complaining about what we don't have and being jealous of people who have more, we should be grateful every day that we have clean water, enough to eat, and roofs over our heads. (By the way, one of the most important benefits of missions trips, that open our eyes to how much of the world lives, is to realize we need to be far better stewards of what God has put in our hands so we can help more people.)

Another problem I see in Christians is the mistaken belief that they can manipulate God to make them wealthy and happy. This is often called the "prosperity gospel," which is the mistaken belief that financial wealth and physical health are always God's will, and positive affirmations and generous donations are sure sources of God's blessings. And on the other hand, the lack of wealth and wellness are signs of God's disfavor.[6] The attention is on doing whatever it takes, using leverage, to get these blessings from God. These pastors and teachers of the prosperity gospel point to passages of Scripture like a lawyer, not like a child of God. They believe they've caught God on a technicality, and He can't escape. What's the problem? They have faith in a God of infinite blessing, but the channel is clogged with their desire to have more for themselves. Oh, they insist they'll give some of it, but they want so much that they won't even notice what they give.

The mentality of scarcity has been a problem in the church for centuries, but the prosperity gospel is a phenomenon where people take kingdom principles and manipulate them for their own gain. The early church was known for generosity of all kinds to all people. In his book, *The Rise of Christianity*, Baylor professor Rodney Stark traces the ups and downs of the church through two millennia. He describes the heart and impact of the believers in the first centuries after Christ's resurrection:

> Christianity revitalized life in Greco-Roman cities by providing new norms and new kinds of social relationships able to cope with many urgent urban problems. To cities filled with the homeless and the impoverished, Christianity offered charity as well as hope. To cities filled with newcomers and strangers, Christianity offered an immediate basis for attachments. To

cities filled with orphans and widows, Christianity provided a new and expanded sense of family. To cities torn by violent ethnic strife, Christianity offered a new basis for social solidarity. And to cities faced with epidemics, fires, and earthquakes, Christianity offered effective nursing services.

God's kingdom strategy of ministering to the suffering was so powerful that other kings took note. In the fourth century a.d., the Roman Emperor Julian tried to launch pagan charities to compete with the highly successful Christian charities that were attracting so many converts. Writing to a pagan priest, Julian complained, "The impious Galileans [i.e., the Christians] support not only their poor but ours as well, everyone can see that our people lack aid from us."[7]

Wouldn't it be terrific if the non-Christians around us were astounded by our care for those in need? I dream of that day!

Have you ever noticed that virtually every item you can buy comes in a range of prices? You can get the budget model, the top-of-the-line model, or a hundred grades in between. And have you noticed that some people (maybe even you and I) generally find a way to rationalize buying the version just one or two above what we can afford? Yeah, it happens. What's that about? Human beings are created with a longing to want more … and more … and more. And Christians are no different. We want more, but when God works deep in our souls to give us His heart for others, our "more" changes. God doesn't just bless us so we can have more for ourselves; He blesses us so we can give more to His causes, including missions, the poor, orphans, widows, and everyone else who needs to know His love. He may appear to them in a dream or send an angel to communicate His message, but far more often, He sends people like you and me to offer our personal presence and care or to offer our resources to fund the presence and care of others. In many ways, things are far different than they were in the Greco-Roman world, but people are still broken and needy. Suffering is still excruciating, and generous hearts are still how God touches lives.

In *The Treasure Principle*, Randy Alcorn puts it clearly: "God prospers me not to raise my standard of living but to raise my standard of giving."[8]

Let me tell you about some people who have raised their standard of giving:

> Justin and Kari had a burning desire to know God and follow Him. They both grew up going to church but were lost in the cares of this world. They knew they had to find a church to teach them and show them what it means to follow Jesus. They came to River Valley, and one Sunday, the message was on giving. The point that hit them was the idea of "counting the cost." Justin wondered, "*What does that even mean?*" Later, he recalled that moment: "It became clear

to me that knowing Jesus, loving Jesus, and obeying Jesus meant giving Him whatever He asks for, no matter what it is. I knew I wouldn't be able to do that if we kept living the way we were living." Before the service was over, Justin turned to Kari, waded through all the things going on in his mind, and said only, "We need to sell our house."

She replied, "Okay!" The Holy Spirit had been showing Kari the same truth that following Jesus required significant changes, so she wasn't too surprised when Justin dropped the bombshell. She remembers, "I had perfect peace and confidence in Justin's leading."

Their small group studied the book *Radical* by David Platt, and at the end, the author challenges readers to commit to sacrificial giving for a year. At about the same time, River Valley was raising money to open another church location (we call them campuses). Justin and Kari prayed about what they should give, and when they came back together to share what God had put on their hearts, each of them had come up with a surprisingly small number. They went back again to ask God for direction, and this time, the number was the same, but Justin told Kari, "This isn't the number God wants us to *give*. It's the number he wants us to *keep*."

Justin went to the bank to transfer money to his checking account, this was going to be the largest amount they had ever given, and he wrote the check for everything except the amount God told them to keep. Before the service that Sunday morning, he and Kari gave the check to one of the ushers and said, "Make sure this gets to the right place."

A few minutes later, one of the pastors stood up and said, "I've got great news! The new campus is fully funded! Praise God!" Kari and Justin knew that day's contributions hadn't been counted yet, so they were confused. They wondered, "What just happened? Did we miss God's voice?" But the pastor continued, "But we have many other projects and many other ways to give. As you know, a hurricane devastated a church where we know the leadership, and we're committed to providing the funds to rebuild the church. The amount we've pledged is ..." The number he put on the screen was the exact amount of the check Kari and Justin had given that morning.

Justin and Kari were surprised that God led them to give so much, surprised that it didn't go to the project they planned it for, and surprised that the amount they gave was exactly what was needed for a group of believers who lived over a thousand miles away. "I'm so grateful," Justin related, "that God brought us on the journey with Him to build His kingdom."

———————

Brian had recently opened his restaurant when COVID hit. Suddenly, he had bills to pay but no prospect of customers. He told his wife, Sarah, "We need to turn the restaurant into a community kitchen. I don't know how we're going to pay for it, and I don't know what we'll do about our staff." He thought he would probably have to declare bankruptcy, but he had an idea. The schools had closed, so the kids who had received free meals were going hungry. Brian wanted to feed those children. He posted on social media that anyone who needed a meal could come to the restaurant to pick one up. Within the first few days, he received around ten thousand requests. They had stocked some food for the opening, but that ran out very quickly. "It was amazing," Brian remembers, "that when one item ran out, someone would bring a replacement through the door. Other restaurants heard what we were doing, so they sent tons (literally) of food to us. Semis loaded with food were parked in front of the restaurant and unloaded."

When those provisions ran out, Brian didn't

know where to turn. The mailman brought a lot of envelopes, and when he opened them, many had cash or checks in them. The total was about $20,000—enough to let them serve for two more weeks. Then, more checks and cash came so they could keep operating. He remembers, "At every point we thought we were done, we leaned into our faith, and God kept telling us, 'I have a way. I have a way.'"

When the COVID restrictions were lifted, people flocked to Brian's restaurant. Crowds stood in line waiting to get in, and his revenues multiplied far beyond what he had expected in the months before COVID. He learned about a restaurant in another country that needed help buying equipment, and Brian was more than glad to provide for the owners. "It's not our money," he explained. "God has blessed us in ways we never imagined."

I met Don years ago when he worked for the Postal Service as a mail carrier. As he attended River Valley and God worked in his heart, he wanted to give himself away in every possible way. He was captivated by stories from our missions trips, and he wanted to go. He used his vacations to travel to places all over the world to build churches, care for orphans, distribute food and supplies, provide eyeglasses, donate Bibles and resources to persecuted churches, and tell people about Jesus. Don and I have gone together to five continents, and each time, he has used God's blessings in his life to bless people. As time passed, the flow only accelerated. I planned to ask him to join our staff team at River Valley, but before I could, he and his wife actually told me that God was leading them in a new direction. Today, Don and his wife are missionaries, serving Jesus in the field. It all started with a heart touched by the limitless love of God.

I want to go back to the passage from Proverbs 11:24: "The world of the generous gets larger and larger; the world of the stingy gets smaller and smaller." God's resources aren't finite. The universe and our concept of His ability to provide are expanding. Nothing is too hard for God. No need is too great, no task too difficult, no prayer too big or small. God is inviting us to join Him on the adventure of generosity. I'm already on it, and I'm asking you to join me. We step into the micro-universe when we stop for a minute to open a door for someone or speak a kind word to a stranger, and we live in the macro-universe when we realize that every time we give a resource—time, money, attention, expertise—in the name of Jesus, the angels celebrate, and God smiles.

Do you feel any resistance to all this? If so, I understand. As I described, I had a misplaced conception for a long, long time. Maybe you grew up in relative poverty, and you want to show God (and everyone else) that you can make it on your own. You have a death grip on every dollar you own. You feel like it's "my money." You need to remember that God has given you the ability to earn wealth and that God's resources aren't a finite pie to divide among people.

Or maybe you grew up in deep poverty and hope God somehow magically provides great wealth for you, like winning the lottery or finding out about a rich uncle leaving you millions. In that case, you need to change your perspective, realize that what you have in your hands is God's gift to you, and begin to live and give generously.

> **God is calling all of us to believe two things: that His resources are limitless, and we thrive when we're open channels to send those resources to those who need Him to show that He cares.**

You may have worked hard for your money, and you don't like the idea of parting with any of it. If you give, it's reluctantly. You need to realize that everything you are and everything you have is a gift from God. Open your hands to receive and give gladly.

You may feel financially vulnerable, and you're afraid that if you give, you'll be left high and dry. Instead of giving to the benevolence ministry, you're afraid you're going to need benevolence. I know people who are elderly and some who are sick who still find ways to be extravagantly generous. There are a lot of generous people who aren't rich.

You may have earned or inherited a substantial amount of money, so you don't have to worry about income and expenses. It's easy to get comfortable … and stay comfortable. But shouldn't life be more than that? Of course it should.

All of us come to God with fears, doubts, and mistaken concepts of His purposes, but we don't have to stay that way. One of the most important signs of spiritual growth is developing a biblical concept of stewardship, not just about money but all resources. You may have little, be middle class or wealthy, old or young, adventuresome or conservative. God is calling all of us to believe two things: that His resources are limitless, and we thrive when we're open channels to send those resources to those who need Him to show that He cares.

Come with me. Discovering a generous life begins the trip of a lifetime. Don't miss it!

chapter three

A Heart Touched by God

A lot of people freak out when a pastor mentions tithing, but I'm not afraid to talk about it. I believe it is the starting point of generosity in the Christian life. To many people, it seems rigid, demanding, and guilt-driven—an antiquated, legalistic requirement that's the very opposite of a heartfelt reflection on God's amazing grace and infinite love. I want to share my perspective on this issue and show that the tithe is a response to hearts being touched by God: relational and not rigid, a delight and not demanding, and love-inspired instead of guilt-driven. For some, the concepts in this chapter will fit with their positive view of God's great-ness and grace; they already get it, and they lean in with a smile on their faces because they've experienced the joy of giving. But for others, the concepts in this chapter may be revolutionary.

At River Valley, we teach a message series about money every year. It's not that we're trying to squeeze every dime from people. It's because we think it's important for believers to get this right. Jesus talked about money and used it as an object lesson a lot: more than Heaven, more than Hell, more than evangelism, and so we need to realize he talked about it a lot! In the Bible, you can find about 500 passages about prayer, 618 about faith, and 2,350 about money.[9] Why? Because our view of money and what we do with it both demonstrates where our hearts are *and* shapes our hearts for the future. In other words, the way we handle money is both a thermometer and a thermostat. As I've said before, it's not really about the money; it's about our hearts.

A heart touched by God gives generously and starts with the tithe. The word *tithe* means "a tenth." Originally, it wasn't focused on religious donations; it was used more generally. We might think most Christians tithe, but let me give you some recent stats: the highest charitable giving was recorded in 2020. That was during the pandemic, and people were motivated to give like never before: $471 billion to U.S. charities, a 5.1 percent increase over the previous year. Since many churches were closed at least some of the year, that meant people had to go to a little more trouble to give. For the first couple of weeks of the lockdown in our area, some people called to ask if they could drive to the church and have a masked person collect a check from them. How do you stand six feet away and take a check from someone leaning out of a car? I'm not sure, but it happened ... a lot. Across the country, those making less than $50,000 a year gave the highest percentage of their income (remember, generous doesn't mean rich), and seven of the ten most generous states were in the South.[10] The giving in 2020 was amazing, but it was a lower percentage than during the Great Depression in the 1930s, and in fact, giving rose 14.9 percent between 1930 and 1931, when the outlook for the economy was particularly bleak.[11] When giving in Europe is compared to the United States, the researchers found that Americans are seven times more generous. The reason for the disparity could be that in Europe, people rely on government assistance more than in our country, so giving doesn't seem as necessary. Probably for a similar reason, Canadians give half as much as Americans.

The most recent statistics reveal that the average family in the U.S. gives $2,514 a year.[12] Twenty-five percent of the people who attend church give nothing. Five percent are regular givers, and they give an average of 2.5 percent of their income. I'm sure the people in our church give more than that, but tithing is the exception rather than the rule. Those who start to tithe usually don't stop at ten percent; they often go on a generosity journey and climb up to twenty percent. If everyone who attends church in America tithed, it would provide an additional $165 billion for the cause of Christ each year. With that money, we could alleviate world hunger, provide clean water, eliminate illiteracy, and fund every missionary.[13]

Some people have told me, "Pastor, I'm a New Testament giver." (Which for many is their way of saying, "I'm not going to give 10 percent but just what I feel is enough.")

I respond, "Fantastic! I'm glad to hear it."

They're surprised at my enthusiasm, so I take a minute to explain my perspective: Jesus always went beyond the Old Testament law. For instance, in His Sermon on the Mount, He taught (I'll paraphrase), "The law says, 'Don't murder,' but I say, 'Don't even be angry.' The law says, 'Don't commit adultery,' but I say, 'Don't lust.' The law says, 'Don't break your oaths,' but I say, 'Just tell the truth.'" So, the law says, "Give a tenth of your income," but Jesus would undoubtedly go beyond that. That's His way. The law was always just a starting point. Those who are captured by the love of Jesus are glad to go beyond that. (When I give "New Testament givers" this explanation, they strangely stop making eye contact.)

Later in Matthew's Gospel, Jesus criticizes the rigid religious leaders about their view of giving: "Woe to you, teachers of the law and Pharisees, you hypocrites! You give a tenth of your spices—mint, dill and cumin. But you have neglected the more important matters of the law—justice, mercy, and faithfulness. You should have practiced the latter, without neglecting the former. You blind guides! You strain out a gnat but swallow a camel" (Matthew 23:23-24 NIV). The Pharisees had been meticulous about giving a tenth of their garden herbs, but they completely missed God's heart. Jesus told them they needed to practice whole-life generosity: the tithe *and* compassion. He said, "You should have ..." That's an imperative to be just, merciful, and faithful, "without neglecting" the tithe. Some people say tithing isn't mentioned in the New Testament. Well, it's right here, and Jesus raised the bar by saying that just giving a tenth isn't enough for a heart touched by God. We go beyond, motivated by Christ's love for those who need justice, mercy, and our faithful involvement in their lives.

Jesus said that if you have two shirts (or tunics), give one away. That's giving 50 percent. When Zacchaeus had lunch with Jesus, his heart was transformed. He committed to give away half of what he owned, and Jesus rejoiced. Jesus ensured people understood that following Him wasn't a casual affair, a buffet to take what we like and ignore what we don't. He told a large crowd, "And whoever does not carry their cross and follow me cannot be my disciple" (Luke 14:27 NIV). We have gold crosses hanging on necklaces and metal ones on the tops of churches, so it's easy to forget that the Romans used crucifixion as the cruelest kind of execution for the worst of criminals. To add to their pain and shame, they had to carry their own crosses to the place where they were nailed to them. That's the analogy Jesus used to describe what it means to give up on our selfish agenda and embrace His agenda! In the same passage, He concludes, "Those of you who do not give up everything, you have cannot be my disciples" (v. 33 NIV). Do I think he means for everyone to do what he told the rich young ruler to do: sell all our possessions and give to the poor? No, but we need to recognize that God is the rightful owner of everything we have, and we're only the stewards. We don't hold our possessions and money in a death grip; we hold Christ closely, and we hold things loosely.

Those who may attend church but don't have a heart touched by God are like a spice that's lost its flavor. Jesus told the crowd, "Salt is good, but if it loses its saltiness, how can it be made salty again? It is fit neither for the soil nor for the manure pile; it is thrown out. Whoever has ears to hear, let them hear" (vv. 34-35 NIV). This isn't a threat or even a prediction. It's just a fact: those who are focused on acquiring as much as they can for their own comfort and pleasure aren't like salt, adding flavor to the lives of the people around them and acting as a preservative to point them to eternal life. "Pay attention!" Jesus is telling us.

What would Jesus say to those of us who live in affluent America and give 2.5 percent? When Paul introduced the need for the Corinthians to give to help the Jerusalem Christians during a famine, he gave them clear instructions: "Now regarding your question about the money being collected for God's people in Jerusalem. You should follow the same procedure I gave to the churches in Galatia. On the first day of each week, you should each put aside a portion of the money you have earned. Don't wait until I get there and then try to collect it all at once" (1 Corinthians 16:1-2). In other words, give regularly. Then, in his second letter, he gives them more encouragement: "Since you excel in so many ways—in your faith, your gifted speakers, your knowledge, your enthusiasm, and your

love from us—I want you to excel also in this gracious act of giving."
He points them again to the love of God as their motivation: "I am not
commanding you to do this. But I am testing how genuine your love is
by comparing it with the eagerness of the other churches." Ultimately,
our giving is a response to God's overwhelming generosity to us: "You
know the generous grace of our Lord Jesus Christ. Though he was rich,
yet for your sakes he became poor, so that by his poverty he could make
you rich" (2 Corinthians 8:7-9). In the same part of the same letter, Paul
encourages the believers in Corinth to contribute to famine relief in
Jerusalem, and he gives them this benchmark: "Each of you should give
what you have decided in your heart to give, not reluctantly or under
compulsion, for God loves a cheerful giver" (2 Corinthians 9:7 NIV).

I've noticed that those who give gain a certain momentum in their
generosity. A flywheel takes a lot of effort to get started, but as it gains
speed, it requires less effort for it to go faster. As people give—and Becca
and I can attest to this—it becomes easier, and in fact, more thrilling to
see God use what we give to change lives. Paul explained, "For God is
the one who provides seed for the farmer and then bread to eat. In the
same way, he will provide and increase your resources and then produce
a great harvest of generosity in you" (2 Corinthians 9:10).

In the narrative of the Bible, we find three eras: before the law was
given, Israel under the law, and the New Testament period of grace. The
three aren't separate. They overlap and interlock, but they have some
distinctions. The tithe was first mentioned long before the law was given,
and it was a response to a blessing. Abraham had fought in a battle
against great odds to rescue Lot, and he had won. Melchizedek, "the king
of Salem and a priest of God Most High," brought Abraham bread and
wine to nourish him, and Melchizedek blessed Abraham:

"Blessed be Abram by God Most High,
　　Creator of heaven and earth.
And blessed be God Most High,
　　who has defeated your enemies for you."
(Genesis 14:19-20)

In response, Abraham gave him "a tenth of all the goods he had recovered" from the battle (v. 20). Abraham wasn't commanded to give a tithe. He gave it spontaneously out of gratitude for God's favor in the fight and His blessing through Melchizedek. Some scholars suggest that Melchizedek was a Christophany, the pre-incarnate Christ who appeared in the form of this priest. The writer to the Hebrews seems to agree, saying, "The name Melchizedek means 'king of justice,' and king of Salem means 'king of peace.' There is no record of his father or mother or any of his ancestors—no beginning or end to his life. He remains a priest forever, resembling the Son of God" (Hebrews 7:2-3). No father or mother or ancestor … that can only describe someone who is preexistent, God himself.

Centuries later, Moses led God's people out of slavery in Egypt and into the wilderness before they entered the Promised Land. During the years they were in the desert, God gave them the Ten Commandments and many more laws to govern every aspect of their new society. The Lord told Moses, "One-tenth of the produce of the land, whether grain from the fields or fruit from the trees, belongs to the Lord and must be set apart to him as holy" (Leviticus 27:30). Holy means "set apart, different from the rest."

We might think that "the Law" was a terrible burden on God's people, establishing unreachable standards and crushing guilt. But when God's people were truly set apart for Him, their adherence to the Law was intended to produce joy and celebration. For example, the Law required that as new crops came in each year, the people were to collect a few "firstfruits" and take them to the priests as an offering to God. It was to be a reminder of how far God had brought them—from 400 years of slavery in Egypt to freedom in the Promised Land. Along with their offering, they were to say:

> "My ancestor Jacob was a wandering Aramean who went to live as a foreigner in Egypt. His family arrived few in number, but in Egypt they became a large and mighty nation. When the Egyptians oppressed and humiliated us by making us their slaves, we cried out to the Lord, the God of our ancestors. He heard our cries and saw our hardship, toil, and oppression. So the Lord brought us out of Egypt with a strong hand and powerful arm, with overwhelming terror, and with miraculous signs and wonders. He brought us to this place and gave us this land flowing with milk and honey! And now, O Lord, I have brought you the first portion of the harvest you have given me from the ground."
> (Deuteronomy 26:5-10)

God, through the Law, wasn't asking for much—the first few grapes or dates or heads of wheat or whatever. But look at the delight intended for those who obeyed:

> Then place the produce before the LORD
> your God, and bow to the ground in worship
> before him. Afterward you may go and cele-
> brate because of all the good things the LORD
> your God has given to you and your house-
> hold. Remember to include the Levites and the
> foreigners living among you in the celebration.
> (Deuteronomy 26:10-11)

Tithing reminded the people of all God had done for them, and they were thrilled! The only command was to invite others to the party!

I can't tell you how many people have told me how God has blessed them when they obeyed Him and began to tithe. Like a father who delights to honor a son's or daughter's glad obedience, God delights to surprise us with blessings we never expected. This isn't a mechanical, vending machine approach: "I give God this much, and He's obligated to give me ten times as much." That's not how loving families operate! Instead, they relate to each other with honor, care, stewardship, and reward. Listen to God speak to people who were facing a lot of stress when the Babylonians threatened them:

> "Bring all the tithes into the storehouse so there
> will be enough food in my Temple. If you do,"
> says the LORD of Heaven's Armies, "I will open
> the windows of Heaven for you. I will pour
> out a blessing so great you won't have enough
> room to take it in! Try it! Put me to the test!
> Your crops will be abundant, for I will guard

> them from insects and disease. Your grapes will
> not fall from the vine before they are ripe," says
> the LORD of Heaven's Armies. "Then all nations
> will call you blessed, for your land will be such
> a delight," says the LORD of Heaven's Armies.
> (Malachi 3:10-12)

Becca and I didn't start tithing when we started a church. We've done this our whole lives—as children, as young adults, and when we worked at jobs before God called us to plant River Valley. Throughout the years, God has abundantly fulfilled the promise in Malachi, opening the floodgates of Heaven to pour out His blessings on us. Sometimes people ask me, "How does it work?"

I reply, "I have no idea, from a natural perspective. I'm not sure that's the best way to think about it. It's more of a relationship than a transaction. God creatively and supernaturally blesses us in different ways and at different times. It's part of the adventure of following Him!"

To illustrate the tithe, when I taught it in a message one weekend, I had our volunteers set up two tables on the stage. First, they brought out ten watermelons. I put one on the Lord's table and the other nine on my table. They brought out acorn squashes, one for the Lord and nine for me. Then cantaloupes, pineapples, bananas, zucchini, eggplants, peppers, oranges, mangos, apples, and lettuce ... one for the Lord and nine for me. (I was hoping they wouldn't bring Brussels sprouts because I'd give the Lord all ten of them.) At the end, my table was overflowing ... but the Lord's table had plenty of room left. My friend Dave Ramsey says, "If you can't live on 90 percent, you can't live on 100 percent. It doesn't require a miracle for you to get through the month."

I then picked up a few things from my table and put them on God's. It didn't really make a difference for me. I still had plenty, but it made the Lord's table more substantial. In other words, I can afford to give more than 10 percent. The noted Baptist pastor, Adrian Rogers, taught, "Give to God what is right, not what is left." Part of what's right is the timing. It's important to give to God first. If we don't, it's easy to get to the end of the month and realize we have nothing left … or maybe just a half-eaten eggplant that we didn't want anyway. I really believe whoever gets the first is honored the most, and I honor God with the tithe and return it to him.

To repeat, the tithe predates the Law, and in the Law, the motivation is delight in responding to God's blessing. When we see how God uses our giving to change lives and provide for

> **I really believe whoever gets the first is honored the most, and I honor God with the tithe and return it to him.**

those in need, we will want to give more. In ancient Israel, God told His people to give another 10 percent for the festivals celebrating the rescue from Egypt and God's faithfulness to His people. And every three years, they gave another 10 percent to care for the poor. It came to about 23 percent of their income. This number is very similar to modern research showing that those who give 10 percent usually increase it to 20.

Sir John Templeton is the founder of Templeton Investments. He has a long track record of investment counseling, and he noted, "I have observed 100,000 families over my years of investment counseling. I always saw greater prosperity and happiness among those families who tithed than among those who didn't." James Kraft, the chairman of the board of Kraft-Phoenix Cheese Corp, claimed, "The only investment I ever made which has paid consistently increasing dividends is the money I have given to the Lord."[14]

Many wonderful organizations do magnificent work locally and around the world, and I applaud them, but God ordains only one organization to represent Him to a lost and dying world—the Church. As God instructed through Malachi, we're to bring our tithes to the storehouse. As I read in the book of Acts, and historical accounts of the early church, I believe the local church is supported by the tithe. At River Valley, we partner with hundreds of organizations, and we let our people know that their money is going far beyond our walls. But the church is God's clearinghouse, the base camp where money goes out to those other ministries. Does that mean it's a sin to give to those organizations? Certainly not, but I'd suggest that the tithe needs to go to your local church, where you attend, serve, invite others to attend and where you are fed regularly. Then, if you want to give to other organizations, give beyond the tithe. Or even better, talk to your pastor and leadership team about your church partnering with outstanding organizations so others in your church can join you in giving to them.

It is a great honor and a solemn responsibility to receive the money people give to the Lord through our church. The gift is holy, not common. It holds immense value to God, not something to take lightly. Sometimes, I hear staff members say, "Now it's time to take the offering," and I tell them, "We're not *taking* anything! We're receiving the tithes and offerings people are giving out of the joy of being blessed by God." I can see on their faces that they want to say, "Hey, Pastor Rob, stop being so particular about a word." But the word is important. They're not giving it to me, and they're not giving it to our church. And we're certainly not taking anything from them! They're giving to God. Our role is to steward the gifts so they are used most effectively for His honor and glory. Nothing less than that. Giving is a form of worship, one that touches God's heart as the Bible tells us, "God loves a cheerful giver," in 2 Corinthians 9:7.

When we give, we give on our debit card or text to give, or if we're old school, we write a check. But our giving must be more than transactional. Give because God has demonstrated His love to you through Jesus paying the ultimate price to rescue you from sin and death. He took the punishment we deserve so we could receive the love and honor He deserves. It's the greatest swap in history! In Genesis 4 and Hebrews 11, we get glimpses of the brothers Cain and Abel. God accepted Abel's offering, but He rejected Cain's, which made Cain so jealous that he murdered his brother. What's that all about? In Hebrews, we learn, "By faith Abel brought God a better offering than Cain did. By faith he was commended as righteous when God spoke well of his offerings. And by faith Abel still speaks, even though he is dead" (Hebrews 11:4 NIV). In what way was Abel's offering "better" than Cain's? The word signifies volume, a bigger number, or greater weight. It may mean that Abel's offering was a tithe, and if not, it certainly was generous, but Cain's was measly. When God applauded Abel, Cain was furious. The amount of each offering was important.

By the way, I'm aware that some pastors encourage people to "start with whatever you can give and then move toward a full tithe." I understand the rationale, but I don't see it in the Scriptures. Nowhere in the Bible is someone affirmed for giving part of the tithe. We teach that ten percent is God's minimum because He never directed us to give less than that, and people need to jump in at that point. It's as much of an adventure for them as it is for others to give so much that they keep only ten percent, and God will bless them for their obedience.

Some people ask, "Why ten percent?" In the Bible, the number ten relates to testing. God tested Pharaoh with ten plagues; He gave His people the Ten Commandments; Jacob complained that his uncle Laban changed his wages ten times. God asks us to test Him to see if He will bless us if we give a tithe, but He's also testing us to see what's in our hearts. Do we grasp the depth of our sin that made us helpless and hopeless apart from Christ? Do we have a strong sense of wonder that the God of glory would stoop to become a human being and suffer the justice we rightly deserve? And do we marvel that when the Father looks at us, He sees the qualities of Jesus that have been credited to us, so He says with all His heart, "This is my beloved son (or daughter) in whom I am well pleased"?

A heart touched by God passes the test. We're thrilled to give because we're amazed that God saved us and adores us. We start with the prelaw tithe like Abraham's gift to Melchizedek (and also Jacob in Genesis 28); we follow the prompts and promises in Leviticus and Deuteronomy, and we graduate to giving even more than the tithe "in view of the mercies of God" (Romans 12:1). He has blessed us so much that we want to be a blessing, not only to other people for Christ's sake but to bless God in thanking Him, worshiping Him, resembling Him, and delighting Him.

When I preach about God's view of finances, I don't assume that everybody is familiar with the concept of the tithe. Many people who are responding to the gospel today have never heard of it, but when grace grips their hearts, they want every aspect of their lives to reflect God's generosity to them. They soon realize God's promises of blessings aren't limited to money. When we love God with all our hearts because He first loved us, He blesses us in all kinds of ways, and our lives abound with gratitude.

Several years ago, on the evening of December 31, a man from our church called me. He said, "Pastor Rob, I need to come to your house right now!"

I asked, "Can't it wait? I'm cooking some of those little hot dogs in barbecue sauce, and they're just about ready. My family is coming over, and we're going to celebrate New Year's together."

"No, Pastor Rob. This can't wait."

"Okay, come on over."

A few minutes later, he rang the doorbell, and I invited him in. Immediately, he launched into his explanation: "Pastor Rob, I just can't shake this. The Lord showed me that I've been living in disobedience. I haven't tithed for years. God spoke to me and said, 'You have to take your check to Pastor Rob at his house tonight.' I made the check to River Valley Church, and God wants me to hand it to you." He gave me a check for $100,000, and then he did something that surprised me. He got on his knees in my living room and asked, "Would you pray for me? I want to live in the grace God has given me and live blessed to be a blessing." I prayed for him. When I finished, he got up, hugged me, and walked out the door. I was stunned, grateful, and so glad I interrupted the little smokies for a heart touched by God!

I hope all those who have not been tithing would respond like this man. No matter the size of the check, give the tithe to the Lord and receive His "Well done, My child!" Get ready for God to put His arms around you and bless you like a loving dad loves his son or daughter.

To those who are consistent with a tithe, be sure to give your first and best to God, not your leftovers. Give to Him first, and then see what happens. Pray, "God, I want to do more for Your glory. May every missionary be fully funded, every hungry person fed, and every orphan secure in a loving environment. And use me to make that happen."

And to those who are giving more than a tithe, way to go! You're responding to the limitless love of God by giving yourself to Him first … and then giving Him even more of your resources. You know it's all about the relationship, and you sense His delight as you give. Keep it up and expand your impact by giving even more.

Outrageous generosity starts with a tithe. But keep going, and you'll be amazed at where the journey takes you. Because over and above the tithe is where the joy of giving really kicks in!

chapter four

Who's In?

In 2005, I attended a pastors' conference and heard a speaker explain how he enlisted people in his church to give above and beyond the principle of tithing. He asked 200 people in his church to consider if they, as individuals or couples, would commit to giving $5,000 to fund projects like building orphanages and churches, digging wells, and providing resources so poor people all around the world could become self-sustaining. He called the concept Kingdom Builders. He used the passage in 2 Corinthians where Paul identifies two huge benefits of giving to famine relief: "So two good things will result from this ministry of giving: the needs of the believers in Jerusalem will be met, and they will joyfully express their thanks to God" (2 Corinthians 9:12). In that case, the people in Jerusalem who were suffering from famine would have resources to buy food, and people would be grateful for God's provision.

As soon as the talk was over, I was in. I told Becca, "This is a great idea! We're bringing this back to River Valley."

We came back home, and I started thinking more about how

Kingdom Builders could be implemented at our church, but I realized there were a couple of problems: First, the threshold of $5,000 was too high for most of our people and probably way too easy for others. Second, having a specific baseline number created more of a club to join than a new way to live. This was so important to me that we modified the concept and taught that the first dollar over the tithe is the start of generosity, and those who give it are Kingdom Builders. Our version isn't about tapping into the wealth of rich people; we want to encourage the generosity of every believer—*everyone* can be a Kingdom Builder.

In the Bible, all four Gospels record the story of a little boy who contributed his lunch of fish and bread so Jesus could multiply it and feed thousands. In our church, he would be a Kingdom Builder. Actually, in his commentary on this Gospel story, William Barclay teaches there were two kinds of miracles that day. He said it is very unlikely that everyone in the crowd had run out of food since at least some of them carried small baskets of kosher food. Many may have already eaten all they had, but some probably still had some food left. One miracle, of course, was when Jesus prayed to bless the boy's lunch and multiplied the loaves and the fish (and I completely believe he did multiply this little boy's meal), and the other miracle may have been people reaching into their baskets and sharing what they had. That was the miracle of generosity. Barclay explains in more detail:

> There may be another and very lovely explanation. It is scarcely to be thought that the crowd left on a nine-mile expedition without making any preparations at all. If there were pilgrims with them, they would certainly possess

supplies for the way. But it may be that none would produce what he had, for he selfishly—and very humanly—wished to keep it all for himself. It may then be that Jesus, with that rare smile of his, produced the little store that he and his disciples had; with sunny faith he thanked God for it and shared it out. Moved by his example, everyone who had anything did the same, and in the end there was enough, and more than enough, for all.

It may be that this is a miracle in which Jesus's presence turned a crowd of selfish men and women into a fellowship of sharers. It may be that this story represents the biggest miracle of all—one that changed not loaves and fishes but men and women.[15]

For Kingdom Builders at River Valley, we created a fund with three designations: local projects, global projects, and developing future Christian leaders. We invite people to pray and ask God for wisdom to set a plan goal, a vision goal, and a dream goal to help do good in all three areas. (As I use this phrase throughout the book, I want to note that we aren't asking for money from people from other churches.)

Because so many people in the world have never heard the Good News of Jesus Christ, our fund spends 50 to 70 percent of the contributions to support missions projects around the world. Almost every time we travel to other lands, we come across amazing organizations, and we're glad to partner with dozens of these vetted ministries involved in meaningful projects: building churches, providing food in famine-stricken areas, distributing Bibles and school supplies, supporting orphanages, digging wells for clean water, and more. We specifically focus on creating opportunities for the 42 percent of the world that has never been presented with the message of Jesus and God's grace through His sacrifice to know they are loved and God's grace can be theirs!

We also designate ten to 30 percent of our Kingdom Builders fund for the growth of local projects through expanding River Valley campuses, planting dynamic churches in our communities, and ministering to the hurting in our cities and neighborhoods. We partner with recovery ministries for adolescents and adults, organizations that plant churches across the nation, prison ministries, and River Valley campus pastors who are planning and constructing new facilities.

We then use ten to fifteen percent of the Kingdom Builders fund to identify and equip the future generation of leaders so they love God, become proficient students of God's Word, and develop strategies to reach the lost and care for the least. We partner with church camps, Bible colleges and universities, youth groups, and other organizations that have demonstrated effectiveness in equipping leaders.

No one is excluded. If a child is given $5 for her birthday, tithes 50 cents, and gives an additional 50 cents, she's a Kingdom Builder. If a student in junior high earns $20 cutting grass, tithes $2, and gives another dollar, he's a Kingdom Builder. If a young couple with two small children earns $80,000 a year in combined salaries, tithes $8,000, and gives $2,400 more, they're Kingdom Builders. If an elderly widow, like my mom, lives on a fixed income, tithes what she earns, and gives $100 more a month, she's a Kingdom Builder.

As I've thought and prayed about this strategy over the years, I realized the best high school football coaches hold clinics to teach younger kids and their coaches the plays they use at the high school level. If they can get little kids who are just starting out in the game to absorb the concepts and strategies at a very basic level, the kids will continue to develop their understanding and skills until they get to high school. That's what I want to happen at our church. I want our youngest children to begin to understand the thrill of being generous and seeing their giving transform lives. We create videos to show and tell what we're doing in all three areas, and we show the videos to all age groups—and not just during the worship services. It's important for children to get a vision of how God might use their generosity to change the world one life at a time.

A few years ago, I realized that we had a bottleneck in this strategy. I asked our kids pastor and youth pastor to meet with me, and I told them, "You're stealing from our church vision!" They looked more than a little surprised, so I explained, "You're not teaching our kids to be generous. They can handle it. I want our little children to be Kingdom Builders, our junior high kids to be Kingdom Builders, and the students in our youth group to be Kingdom Builders. Got it?" I explained that it wasn't about the amount but about establishing a foundation God could build on in shaping the direction these kids were going. They realized they hadn't given this effort enough attention, apologized for giving less than their best, and committed to make the changes. Our little children raise money every year for Boys and Girls Missionary Clubs to provide resources to minister to kids around the world. Our youth group supports a ministry called Speed the Light to

> It's important for children to get a vision of how God might use their generosity to change the world one life at a time.

buy vehicles for missionaries—cars, yes, but not always. In some cultures, they might need a yak, a boat, a bicycle, or a bus. The young people raise money for all that—and get to celebrate together when God uses them to meet these important needs!

Many people underestimate what young people are able to give. I think that's a big mistake! We see with platforms like Youtube and TikTok (I'm not on it, but I've heard about these stories) kids are making hundreds of thousands or even millions of dollars. Some resell sneakers; others do odd jobs, but they don't want to be left out. Just last year, our youth and kids gave over $1 million dollars combined to the projects I just mentioned. As their pastor, I couldn't be more proud of them!

Do we want rich people to participate? Absolutely! They have a God-given, phenomenal opportunity to use their wealth to advance the kingdom in big ways, but they're not better than anyone else whose heart has been touched by God's generosity to them and becomes generous in response. In fact, those who are the most generous usually aren't the ones who give a lot out of their abundance. They're the people who give so much they must make significant adjustments in their lifestyles. They count the cost and conclude it's worth it.

When my son Logan was thirteen, we had a very instructive conversation. He was into cars, and on a Sunday morning, he saw a man drive into our parking lot in a BMW that cost well over $100,000. Logan told me, "Dad, did you see that man's car? It's so expensive. I'm glad he comes to our church so he can be a Kingdom Builder and give a lot to missions!"

I wanted to tell him, "Son, that man has never given a dime to our church," but I thought twice and told him, "Just because someone has a nice car doesn't mean they're a great Kingdom Builder. You can't judge from appearances who's generous." In the same way, you can't judge from appearances who is wealthy. Someone driving a BMW could be neck-deep in car payments and debt. And someone living in a modest house could be a multi-millionaire who chooses to invest their wealth elsewhere. Our generosity—or lack of generosity—is between each of us and our Creator.

On the other end of the spectrum of hearts for God, let me tell you about some of our church's Kingdom Builders:

> A family with three daughters caught the vision for generosity, and the girls had an idea about how to raise money. They bought material and made scarves out of yarn that were very labor intensive and very creative. They sold them to family, friends, neighbors, and even at church gatherings and their parents' workplaces. They raised over $5,000.

> When my son Connor was twelve, he was scheduled to go with me on a missions trip to Eswatini, a landlocked little country in southern Africa. He came up with the idea of asking people in our church to donate pocket change so he could use it to help the people of Eswatini. I asked, "Son, why don't you ask them for folding money—for their dollars?"
>
> He replied, "Dad, a lot of people want to keep their bills, but everybody will give me their

change." He was right, so a new idea was born that day.

We held a "Change the World Sunday" and asked people to dig into their pockets and purses. We gave everybody a plastic bag and asked them to come back the next week with their change in it. They brought about $2,000 the next Sunday. When we went on our trip, the church leaders in Eswatini used the money Connor had raised to produce blueprints for an orphanage and a facility to provide feeding care. They then approached the king of the country, showed his team their plans, and asked him to provide crown land. God moved, and he agreed to gift them enough land for everything they had the vision to build. This remarkable new site was made possible, in part, by a young boy with a vision to use money to advance God's kingdom in a foreign land. When we showed up several years later to dedicate the new buildings, we discovered that the church leaders had named the land "Connor Field." I'm sure Connor was excited, but as his dad, I was overwhelmed. River Valley's "Change The World Sunday" has continued and now the offering is over $40,000 from all the change and donations!

When Sam was just thirteen, God called him to be an entrepreneur. He wanted God to bless him so he could be a blessing. He remembers, "God had knocked on the door of my heart, so I knocked on the door of every house in our neighborhood. I asked if they would hire me to cut their grass. That summer, I made about $1,000. Before school started, I sensed God say that He wanted me to give it all to Kingdom Builders for Speed the Light. I knew God would multiply what I was giving. I told Him, 'Lord, I'll go where You want me to go, and I'll be who You want me to be. I know this first gift is just the beginning. I'm Yours.'"

A few months later, the Lord brought a couple of mentors into Sam's life, and he started his first company making t-shirts. In just a year and a half after starting the company, he brought in over $50,000 in sales and gave over $15,000 to Kingdom Builders. He relates, "What I like about Kingdom Builders is that every dollar touches hearts. When we give to expand God's kingdom, the impact is eternal.

(As I write this, I'm sure thousands of churches want a youth group filled with teenagers like Sam!)

Cory and Deb probably don't fit the profile you've imagined for Kingdom Builders. When they learned about its impact, they prayed, "Lord, what would You have us do to be a part of this?" They set a vision goal for the first year and doubled it each year for four years. The next year, they had a family meeting with their two children and told them, "This is the year of sacrifice."

Deb had been diagnosed with multiple sclerosis a few years earlier, and the disease was rapidly progressing and becoming much more challenging (she required the use of a cane to walk). Halfway through their year of sacrifice, God spoke to Deb that it was time for her to resign from her job. She and Cory realized this wasn't the kind of sacrifice they were expecting. With her loss of income, they didn't see any way they could meet their vision goal for the year.

On Deb's last day at the office, their financial advisor called with some surprising news. He said, "I'm not sure you know this, but you're covered by a long-term disability policy."

Deb recalls, "That wasn't part of the equation. God just said, 'Walk away from your job.'"

The first official notice that the policy was in effect was a check in the mail. The check and the money from the policy for the next few months were enough for Deb and Cory to meet their giving goal for the year. Cory and Deb sat in their living room with their children, marveling at what God had done. Deb relates, "Cory and I have seen God do amazing things when we trust Him."

———

I was at a conference and had a free night for dinner. I asked someone I had just met the night before if he had plans for dinner, and he was open and accepted my invitation. (Both our wives couldn't make the trip and we were some of the few people there without their spouses. I hate eating alone, so I'm glad he said yes!) He is the CEO of one of the largest companies in Texas, and I shared the principles of plan-vision-dream (more on that in the next chapter) and what it means to be a Kingdom Builder. After only a few minutes, he sat back in his chair and told me, "I've never heard anything like this. It's going to give me a new way to live … for the rest of my life. I'm going to do this." He had never had a dream goal to give to God, and now he lives with a dream of what God can do with his business skills.

———

A pastor friend of mine asked me to share the concepts of plan-vision-dream with a couple of business owners at his church. He knew I loved to golf, so we met at Top Golf so we could hit some golf balls while we talked. My friend had prepped them to be ready for my explanation, and once they heard it, they were ready to jump in with both feet. They loved the idea of plan-vision-dream, and they both made a commitment to be Kingdom Builders for the rest of their lives. As we left the driving range, both men gave me huge bear hugs. That's not the normal reaction when I take guys to Top Golf, but it's becoming the norm when I help men and women realize what it means to be a Kingdom Builder.

I don't want to give the impression that giving above the tithe is always easy. It's not. It requires sacrifice and hard choices. This level of generosity asks a lot from every person who wants to be a Kingdom Builder, from kids to adults, from those who are barely scraping by to the super wealthy. Our culture pushes us to compare what we have with those who have more than us, so we're always coming up short ... and we believe we need to catch up! But this is different. It's rearranging our priorities from getting to giving, from comfort to impact, from living for ourselves to living for Jesus and others.

This is a new way of thinking, praying, and living. It's the only way I want to live, and as I've invited people to join me, thousands have gotten on board when they realized Kingdom Builders is more than a program or ministry. It's a way to become someone who intentionally lives, works, serves, and gives to build the Kingdom of God. Maybe your church doesn't use the term Kingdom Builders, but surely your pastor has vision for what God could do through your generosity? Maybe you used to tune out during the part of the service when giving was talked about. Or maybe you've felt your part isn't significant enough. Can I challenge you? Talk to your pastor, look for causes and organizations that move your heart. Don't plug your ears because you're worried you'll feel moved to give, but ask God to help you be a blessing every time your heart is moved.

The title of this chapter is "Who's In?" I don't want anyone to miss the opportunity to be able to say, "I'm in" in their relationship with God. It's easy to miss the grace of God. Many people think that they're pretty good people who just need a little help from God to be acceptable, but that misses the point! Yes, some of us are obviously more sinful than others, but sin comes in all shapes and sizes, and in fact, the people who completely missed the heart of Jesus were those who were sure they weren't only pretty good, but they were very good. We can miss God's heart in two very different ways: by turning our backs on Him by being so bad or by trusting that we're so good. The teaching of Scripture is that "Everyone has sinned: we all fall short of God's glorious standard" (Romans 3:23). All of us need a Savior. "For God presented Jesus as the sacrifice for sin. People are made right with God when they believe that Jesus sacrificed his life, shedding his blood … God did this to demonstrate his righteousness, for he himself is fair and just, and he makes sinners right in his sight when they believe in Jesus" (vv. 25-26).

It's like this: If you lined up every person on the planet at the edge of the Grand Canyon and told them they had to jump across, some would do better than others. Most of us would make it about five feet. The world record for the long jump was set by Mike Powell in 1991 at just over 29 feet. Have you ever been to the Grand Canyon? Have you ever seen pictures of it? Then you know that even the very best of us fall pitifully short in our ability to jump across. It's the same with our need for Jesus. We couldn't save ourselves by our goodness, but on the other hand, none of us is beyond the reach of God's grace. When we transfer our trust from ourselves and our efforts to Jesus and His sacrifice for us on the cross, something amazing happens. Paul described it in his letter to the Colossians: "For he has rescued us from the kingdom of darkness and transferred us into the kingdom of his dear Son, who purchased our freedom and forgave our sins" (Colossians 1:13-14). We change our primary citizenship! We still live on Earth and in our country, but our true home is God's kingdom.

How does someone experience this rescue and identity transfer? By grace (God's remarkable compassion and favor drawing you to Christ) through faith. In another letter, Paul explained, "God saved you by his grace when you believed. And you can't take credit for this; it is a gift from God. Salvation is not a reward for the good things we have done, so none of us can boast about it" (Ephesians 2:8-9). You can express this faith in prayer, something like this:

> Lord Jesus, I need You. I've been trying to run my own life, and it's not working. Thank You for taking my place and paying the price I deserved to pay for my sins. And thank You for making me a citizen of Your Kingdom. I want

to experience all the love You want to pour out
on me. I want to live for You.

The grace of God isn't something we experience only when we cross the boundary line from one kingdom to another. It's the way we relate to God all day, every day. He never stops being gracious to us, and as we realize it more and more, our lives are filled with increasing levels of gratitude and generosity. There's nothing like it in the universe. Are you in?

chapter five

Plan-Vision-Dream

Back in 2010, I was in Kenya on a missions trip with eight other pastors to see the progress of projects we'd supported in the past and check out other promising possibilities. We saw churches we'd helped build, food distribution networks, and schools using supplies we'd provided. We were, as they say, "out in the sticks," far from Nairobi, the nation's capital. This is where God changed my lifetime strategy for generosity.

It was almost 10:00 in the morning when we arrived at a village where we'd given money to pay for food because many of the children were malnourished. A couple of adults were mixing what looked like oatmeal in a children's pool near the classroom, which I thought was odd because it was long past normal breakfast time. Even odder, very few children were there. I asked one of the adults where they were, and he said, "The children will be arriving very soon."

I commented, "You start school very late here." (Call me Captain Obvious.)

The man smiled and explained, "We have to wait for the lions to go to sleep."

With my usual reserve, I almost shouted, "What? Lions?!"

He smiled again. "Yes, lions hunt at night and into the early morning. It's not safe for children to walk here while the lions are on the prowl."

Before long, enough kids had come for us to start serving breakfast. I asked if I could scoop the oatmeal from the kiddie pool into their bowls. As each child came by, I used a little red cup to serve their portion. As each one thanked me, tears welled up in my eyes. When we finished, I turned to one of the pastors and said, "Man, we've got to find ways to fund more of these projects. This is making a difference!" I asked the man who had prepared the oatmeal if I could keep the red cup to remind me of that morning and the need to feed more children. I also wanted it to be a constant reminder that God has blessed me to be a blessing. The cup is featured prominently in my office so I can see it often and remember.

The next day, the other pastors and I traveled to visit an orphanage led by Clive and Mary Beckingham. The facility includes several nice buildings on a couple of acres. As we talked, I learned that it's a multi-site orphanage. I was amazed at the vision and leadership of this couple because they were just normal people, not superstars. I asked them to tell their story. Clive began, "Mary and I had a plan, and we came to Kenya and just worked the plan. We just bought a small home and took in orphans. One day we had a ceremony for a couple who adopted one of our little boys. A man who had come to celebrate with the couple walked up to me and said, 'Clive, what you're doing is amazing. The adoptive father is my best friend. This is the happiest day for my friend and his wife. If there's anything I can do for you to say thank you, please let me know.'"

Clive wasn't sure what the man was offering, so he just thanked him, but the man wasn't finished. He asked, "Do you have a vision for your orphanage?"

"Yes. Actually, yes, I do," Clive responded. "Wait right here." Clive went into the house and, a minute later, came out with a set of blueprints. He unrolled them and told the man, "This is my vision. We want to expand the orphanage so we can care for more children." Clive pointed to several places and said, "I want a building here ... and here ... and here."

The man's eyes beamed, and he told Clive, "You won't believe this, but I own one of the largest construction companies in the country. As a thank-you gift, I'm going to build those buildings for you ... for free." Clive was, of course, thrilled. A minute or two later, the man added, "By the way, I'm not a Christian, but I'm very glad to help." God had moved in the heart of man who wasn't even a Christian to expand the impact of a Christian orphanage. God surely works in mysterious ways!

Construction started right away, and before long, Clive and Mary were caring for more children. Several years after the man committed to the project, he came back to meet with the couple. This time, he asked,

"Do you have a dream? What can you imagine as the greatest impact you can have?"

Clive told him, "Yes, absolutely. I want to start more orphanages all across Kenya."

The man replied, "I have several buildings I'm not using in different rural areas of the country. Go ahead and pick out a few of them; they're all yours."

As Clive related this story to me, he was surprised that I was so excited about it. I told him, "This is what captures people's hearts and propels their generosity. Your story is magnificent, and God is going to use it in amazing ways." Little did I know how much.

As the other pastors and I rode away on the bus, I was overwhelmed with what I'd seen. I sensed the whisper of the Spirit: "This is the way I want you to live and give from today through the rest of your life." I realized Clive's conversation with the builder followed a path: plan, vision, dream.

God loves for people to make plans as long as we trust Him as we make them, and we know that He may change them.

God loves for people to make plans as long as we trust Him as we make them, and we know that He may change them. In one of his psalms, David prayed, "May he grant your heart's desires and make all your plans succeed" (Psalm 20:4). And wise King Solomon instructs us, "Commit your actions to the Lord, and your plans will succeed" (Proverbs 16:3).

Plans are essential, but they're not enough. God wants us to have a vision of how we can have a bigger impact on Him in the growing spheres of influence, starting with our families and moving beyond to our neighbors, our communities, and countries around the world. A plan focuses on using the resources you have in your hands, but a vision looks beyond your own resources to have a much deeper, wider impact. We need faith in both, but we need more faith in the vision. The writer to the Hebrews explains, "And it is impossible to please God without faith. Anyone who wants to come to him must believe that God exists and that he rewards those who sincerely seek him" (Hebrews 11:6). He then describes the amazing impact of people who believed God for more. You may be familiar with the proverb: "Where there is no vision, the people perish" (Proverbs 29:18 KJV), but it may be more instructive to look at a different translation: "When people do not accept divine guidance, they run wild. But whoever obeys the law is joyful" (NLT).

The prophet Habakkuk lived during one of the most difficult times in Israel's history, when the Babylonian armies threatened to destroy the temple and the nation. Even in the middle of his prophecy of doom, he offered God's people strong hope for a better future. To be sure they didn't forget, he told them to write it down:

> Then the Lord said to me,
> "Write my answer plainly on tablets,
>> so that a runner can carry the correct
> message to others.
> This vision is for a future time.
>> It describes the end, and it will be fulfilled.
> If it seems slow in coming, wait patiently,
>> for it will surely take place.
>> It will not be delayed." (Habakkuk 2:2-3)

We may think that a vision is something that's so "out there" that it's beyond anything we can reasonably expect, but the object of our faith is the infinite power, wisdom, and love of Almighty God. When God puts a vision of something much bigger than ourselves in our hearts, we need to honor it by writing it down, describing it in as much detail as we can, and trusting that someway, somehow, sometime, God will fulfill it. As I said, a plan relies on what's in our hands, but a vision depends on what God has in His hands.

A dream is bigger than a vision and requires even more of God's miraculous power. We need to hold our dreams close to our chests. My suggestion is don't tell anyone except your spouse if you're married. Wait for the Lord to begin putting the pieces in place, and *then* share your dream with others. One of the most painful stories in the Bible is of a young man, Joseph, who shared two dreams with his parents and brothers, after which he was thrown into a pit, sold into slavery, falsely accused of sexual assault, and languished in a dungeon for many years. Only then did God fulfill the dream, but not at all the way Joseph had expected. I learned

> A plan relies on what's in our hands, but a vision depends on what God has in His hands.

this when I shared the dream of our church. I shared that we would one day be a thousand people and give one million dollars to world missions. People would pull me aside and tell me, "Don't say that, it may not happen, you sound crazy or even arrogant!" The lesson: don't share your dream with non-dreamers! It will sound insane to them and maybe even offensive because they believe it's all about *your* fame and power. A God-given dream is so huge that it can't be about us—it's always about Him.

How does this process of plan-vision-dream play out in our generosity? God gave us a baseline for our giving of ten percent, which is the tithe. Generosity, at least the way I'm describing it in this book, is our giving *beyond* the tithe, "over and above."

For the *plan* for generosity, I ask people, "What can you do today with the blessings God has already put in your hands? How can you reorganize your income and expenses so His blessings in your life right now can be more of a blessing to others?" People evaluate their finances and create a plan, either for additional monthly giving, a one-time gift, a monthly commitment or something more creative like stocks or property. It may be $20 more a month, or it could be an asset worth millions. In any case, it's giving resources they already control. For you and me, whatever it is, simply work the plan.

The *vision* for generosity stretches us to trust God to provide a yearly gift or commitment beyond what we have or expect to have. If the plan was to give an additional $2,400 a year, maybe the vision is to double that this next year. Many people are fearful of taking this step because it requires faith, but don't miss the excitement of stepping out in faith and believing that God will provide. Ask God for guidance, write down what He puts on your heart, and pray faithfully that He'll provide and fulfill the vision. Now a *dream* is a mind-expanding, faith-challenging, someday goal that's on the edge of crazy (or maybe a little beyond it). When God puts a dream for giving in your heart, your instant response may well be, "No way!" But over time, God continues to prod you, and sooner or later, you're convinced His dream is becoming your dream. Again, it may be an amount of money that's a multiple of what you've given in the vision, or it could be the resources to fund an entire project that's on your heart. It could be a gift that changes the lives of thousands, but no matter the amount, it's such a joy to live with a dream goal for your generosity!

Let me stop right here for a minute. A businessman who heard these concepts told me, "Pastor Rob, you realize you have this backward, don't you? In my world, people are challenged to dream big, let that crystalize into a clear vision, and then craft a workable plan to make it a reality. So ..."

He didn't have to complete his sentence. I knew exactly what he was saying. I explained, "You're exactly right. The dream-vision-plan model is how most people think, but plan-vision-dream is a spiritual progression to believe in God for ever-increasing impact. I think of the debt-snowball method when paying off consumer debt. Most say to pay off the highest interest rate debt first because it makes sense on paper. But what it leaves out is that personal finance is way more about our behavior than the math! We are wired to see a small victory and let it build into a larger one. We need to learn to walk before we can run, and we have to run before we can fly. In this model, God increasingly expands our faith, so we trust Him for more." I told him that the Kingdom of God is diametrically different from how the world works. It's upside down: The last shall be first; to save your life, you must lose it, and those who want to be great must be the servants of all. (This means to live for God and heaven as your reward, and not for this short life on earth.) It's inside out. It's not what goes into us that defines us but what comes from our hearts; genuine change happens inside and is demonstrated by visible fruit. It's backward forward: instead of focusing only on what we can get now, our much bigger view of the glory of Heaven shapes our present values, purposes, and choices. Yes, plan-vision-dream is backward, just like the most important principles in the Bible. (And when we realize God is in control of it all, we discover His way is forward, not backward.)

He nodded and told me, "Okay, I get it." He was on board and became an advocate of the process.

Plan-vision-dream isn't some obscure, unreachable concept. Since

God taught me plan-vision-dream in Kenya, I knew this would be the way we taught our congregation. We teach the principles of plan-vision-dream, and we identify worthy projects—in our backyards and across the globe—that capture our hearts and give us a multiplied impact for Christ. In our experience, our efforts through Kingdom Builders have proven to be one of the most exciting, fulfilling, challenging, and faith-building things we've ever done. This isn't just a bucket where people put money; it's a community of individuals and families who prayerfully commit to giving generously to provide local impact, fuel global missions, and develop future leaders.

Some churches use "faith promise" campaigns to ask people to give more. If you're not familiar with that, the church asks people to write down an amount "by faith" that they intend to give to the campaign. Sometimes they fulfill that amount, and other times they give what they can. I've found that people are hesitant to commit to these types of campaigns. That's not what I ask our church to do. The motivation isn't to meet some arbitrary financial goal. We don't give our people an individual target; we ask them to pray and ask God what He wants them to give. In this way, they tap into the deep well of God's blessings in their lives and trust Him to use them to bless others with what's already in their hands, what God already has in His hands, and even beyond that to accomplish something that makes the angels sing!

A dream is a mind-expanding, faith-challenging, someday goal that's on the edge of crazy (or maybe a little beyond it).

Some people who hear about Kingdom Builders assume the people involved are all rich and give millions out of their great wealth, but that's not the case. People at every income level and every walk of life have trusted God to lead them in it. Every person can participate. It's not about the money in their pockets or bank accounts; it's about their desire to sacrifice for Christ, who sacrificed himself for them. It's not for rich people; it's for generous people. For instance:

> Park is a young man in our youth group. When he learned about plan-vision-dream, God gave him a vision to give $500 to the church. He wasn't looking only at his allowance; he trusted God to go far beyond his limited means. His parents, close friends of ours, weren't too confident that he could meet that goal, and they imagined coming to the end of the year and writing a check for close to $500 to make up the difference. They shouldn't have worried. Park didn't just raise the $500; he went way over that and gave $1,100. His faith and his desire to give more showed him and his parents that God has more than enough in His hands when we live generously.

———

A couple in our church learned about plan-vision-dream, but they had no idea how God might fulfill the vision He put on their hearts: $7,500 above their tithe. This was a huge stretch, but they clearly believed God had directed them to give it. In previous years, when COVID hit, the government had sent stimulus checks, which they had given to Kingdom Builders. Now the government checks were over, and God had asked them to believe for way more than a COVID check. They wondered, *How will God provide?* One Sunday they asked God to provide the money, then wrote down their vision and prayed. The following Friday, the wife looked at their checking account, and it had $7,500 extra in it. She called her husband at work and told him the money had come from his company. She asked, "What is this? Where did it come from?" He didn't know, so he went in to talk to his boss. The boss didn't know either, so he contacted the owner of the company. When the boss asked about the $7,500 deposit, the owner told him, "On Monday morning, I felt guilty that I haven't given bonuses for the last two years, so I told our accountant to transfer money immediately to every employee's account and give them a bonus." The couple had a vision that was more than they could manage on their own, so they prayed on a Sunday. The next day, God put it on the company owner's heart to give bonuses, and by Friday, the money—the exact amount they'd committed to give—was in their account! The couple was thrilled to write a check to Kingdom Builders. Now they're excited to see what God will do next in their generosity adventure!

Becca and I are huge fans of Kingdom Builders because of the incredible good it does in our local area and around the world. From the beginning, we've planned to give above our tithe. (I'm going to practice what I preach in this area and not just expect others to do it.) God has given us a vision to give even more, and we have a new dream that we're not telling anyone about yet. We cut back on our expenses so we could give a significant amount each year to Kingdom Builders, and we've built on that amount annually. One year, as I prayed and asked God for a vision amount, I felt He wanted us to give $10,000 more than we were giving. When I told Becca, she was wondering if I really felt the number was right and if I had any idea where the $10,000 would come from. Just like so many people, we tried to come up with a plan in our own efforts.

I told her, "This is a vision. God wants us to increase our giving by $10,000. I don't know how He'll make it happen, but I'm sure He will."

Becca said, "Well then, let's write the vision down and believe God for it."

Two weeks later, I received a call from a nonprofit organization in Indiana. The director explained their purpose and impact, and he asked me to join their board. I told him, "Thanks for the offer, but I'm already on too many boards."

He didn't take no for an answer. He explained, "This organization was started and is funded by several businessmen. They began a new business because they want to give millions from their business revenues to missions. And by the way," he added offhandedly, "we give board members $10,000 a year to give to any charity of their choice."

Suddenly, I was very interested! I asked, "Could I give the money to a ministry of our church called Kingdom Builders? It gives money to projects in the U.S. and around the world. Could I give the money for that?"
He assured me, "Of course. That's perfect."

I wanted to shout, "Are you kidding me? That's exactly what Becca and I have been praying for. I'm in!" But instead, I tried to be calm and professional and simply said,

"Thank you, I'm happy to accept, when is the Board meeting?"

How did God fulfill the vision He gave Becca and me? Twenty years ago, several guys sat in a restaurant and drew a business plan on a napkin with the goal of making enough money to give millions to the cause of Christ. Two decades later, I got a call from someone I didn't know about an organization I'd never heard of to ask me to be on their board. Their yearly stipend for board members was the way God answered our prayers to be able to give more. What's even more exciting is that they are doing so well and giving millions annually to missions that each board member now gets $25,000 to direct to a charity … and all of mine goes to Kingdom Builders! It was in His hands, and Becca and I simply had to believe God to put it in our hands so we could be generous.

Another couple in our church are business owners who got excited when they learned about plan-vision-dream. The husband told his wife, "Our plan could be to give $250,000 right now."

She didn't hesitate: "Let's do it!"

He then said, "Let's do this now, and then trust God with a vision to give $500,000 a year."

She asked, "How long do you think it will take for the company to grow so we can do that?"

"About five years," he responded.

But something supernatural took place, and within 18 months, they were able to give their vision amount of $500,000 above their tithe to Kingdom Builders—much sooner than they expected. But it gets better! Just two years later, they asked Becca and me to go to dinner. As soon as we sat down, the husband teared up. He told us, "Pastor Rob and Becca, we can't believe we're at this point. We started with a plan, then God gave us a vision, and tonight, we want to tell you that God has fulfilled our dream—we're giving a $1,000,000 check to Kingdom Builders."

All four of us were crying in celebration of what God had done in such a short time. Then I asked with tears flowing down my face, "What's your *new* dream?!"

He laughed and said, "I can't tell you. Remember? It's our secret." (He got me on that one.) But then he told us anyway, "We want to give $1,000,000 to Kingdom Builders every year for the rest of our lives."

I quickly responded, "I pray you live to be a hundred!" (I can't believe I said that.)

That was five years ago. This couple has given at least that much every year to Kingdom

Builders, and they've started a new ministry to challenge business owners to live differently— not to make a lot of money to spend on luxuries, but to make a lot of money to spend advancing the Kingdom of God. Instead of buying another expensive house or fancy car or otherwise splurging on themselves, they store up treasure in Heaven where moths and rust can't destroy (Matthew 6:20). They can fill Heaven with people who point back to them with hearts full of gratitude because they consider others more important than themselves. They can build a church in Kenya, dig a well in India, rescue young girls from sex trafficking, help drug addicts in our own cities, or even provide a school and food for kids in the Philippines … and there are a thousand other ways God is using them to touch lives for His glory.

Plan-vision-dream has captured the hearts of the rich and the not-so-rich, young and old, people in our neighborhoods, and those on the other side of the world. All these people I've described are just a few of the many who've discovered God's idea to revolutionize our motivations so we want what He wants. We care about the people He loves—*all* of his children. This is a new way of living, adding a deeper level of intentionality to giving. I've had the pleasure of watching people who enjoy the thrill of seeing God come through so they can have a far greater impact than they ever dreamed possible. To them, to me, and, hopefully to you, it's about much more than money. It's about being Jesus's partner in rescuing the lost, providing for the poor and the outcasts, building His kingdom, and growing in our faith. There's not a hint of guilt or pressure. Plan-vision-dream

Instead of buying another expensive house or fancy car or otherwise splurging on themselves, they store up treasure in Heaven where moths and rust can't destroy.

is an opportunity and a challenge to live for more than ourselves and then to trust God to make us "blessed to be a blessing." God continues to enrich us so we can be more generous than we ever imagined. When that happens, people's lives are transformed, we're thrilled beyond words, and God rejoices with us. If you're not already doing it, I pray you find the faith and joy in going over and above the tithe with a plan, a vision, and a dream for your generosity!

chapter six

Giving Is a Muscle

In the early years of River Valley Church, we were growing, but we were still in a rented warehouse space. I had big plans to buy property, and I wanted our people to save their money in preparation for when I'd ask them to dig deep and sacrifice to finance the new building. During those years, we had frequent special offerings for missionaries, organizations that were our partners, and special projects, but as I asked people to give to those things, in the back of my mind, I was thinking, "*Don't give* too *much! Save for later.*" (I still believed there was a finite pie, like I described in Chapter 2.)

But one day in prayer, I sensed God saying, "I'm going to show you some things about giving. I want you to invite a missionary to feature every weekend in December."

I replied, "Every weekend in December?" You see, if you've grown up in the church at all, you know that when a missionary visits and speaks, the congregation typically takes up an offering to support their ministry. We already had a Christmas Eve offering planned for the pastors' bonuses. At the time, we had five pastors on our team, and this was our way to give them a year-end blessing. "Lord," I thought, "if we ask people to give to the missionaries, there won't be anything left for us." Despite my doubts, I was obedient to this prompting of the Holy Spirit and lined up the missionaries.

On the first Sunday in December, the first missionary spoke, and I asked people to give to that ministry. I didn't hold back because I wanted to be fully obedient to God. The offering was really good. When the second missionary came the next week, I thought, "*Tough break for you. Our people gave a lot last week, so there's not much left.*" But the special offering that week was even higher. I was really surprised, but I concluded, "*Oh, I get it. People were more interested in that ministry than the one the week before.*" When we started the service on the third Sunday, I looked at the missionary couple and thought, "*Oh man, they have no shot. Our well is dry by now.*" But I was wrong. Really wrong. Our people gave even more than the previous week!

A few days later, we held our Christmas Eve services. Obviously, I hadn't learned a thing. I was sure the offering for the pastors' bonuses would be paltry, but it was the largest ever. I hadn't begged or put extra pressure in the appeal. I just presented the opportunity to bless our young staff. I wondered, "*How in the world did that happen? It doesn't make sense.*"

I sensed the Lord downloading a message straight to my heart: "Giving is like a muscle. The more you use it, the stronger it gets."

I try to stay in shape by working out. Every time I use weights, like a bench press, by the end of the reps, my muscles feel like they're completely drained. I'm spent, weak, and sore. But in fact, breaking down muscles makes them stronger. (To be honest, getting stronger isn't my primary motivation for working out. I want to burn calories so I can eat more, but don't tell anybody at my fitness center.)

People who regularly work out establish a rhythm that works for them. For instance, many who want to work on strength and cardiovascular fitness work out five days a week: three days of strength training, two for cardio, and two days of rest. At our church, we follow a rhythm each month for Kingdom Builders projects: ask, update, celebrate, and rest. Here's

> Giving is like a muscle. The more you use it, the stronger it gets.

how it works: On the first Sunday of the month, we feature the project or mission we're highlighting (like an orphanage, sex trafficking rescue, or building a church in an underdeveloped country), and we ask for a specific amount of money. The ask is illustrated by photos or a video so people can see the reality of the need. The second Sunday, we share an update on the contributions from the previous week. The third Sunday, we celebrate how God is using the generosity of our people (whether we met our goal or not, people were still generous) and offer one last opportunity to give to the project. On the fourth Sunday, we rest, which means we don't talk about any of our projects. The following month, we choose another ministry, missionary, or project, and we start the rhythm again. In this way, we maintain an effective, regular emphasis on Kingdom Builders.

We exercise our giving muscle by giving generously above the tithe, and like working out with weights, the regular exercise of giving provides additional strength to give more. A woman in our church called to ask a question about her tithe. She said, "I've been giving every month by direct deposit, but I don't feel it any longer. I'm thinking about stopping that method and writing a check each month. Does that sound reasonable?"

I responded, "No, I wouldn't change your method of giving. You've gotten to a point where tithing is easy. Maybe it's time to ask God to give you a plan for additional giving this year, a vision for what He might do so you can give even more and a dream of having a phenomenal impact on the kingdom. Instead of seeing the tithe as the end, let it be the beginning of your generosity journey and go up from there!"

She hadn't considered giving more than a tithe, but this conversation propelled her to a new level of generosity. Her giving muscle was getting stronger because it was being regularly used.

When you've reached the goal of regular tithing, how do you know what generosity looks like? Where do you start? What's the first step in becoming a Kingdom Builder even before plan-vision-dream? When I travel, I use the gym in the hotel to stay in shape. Of course, the machines are different from the ones at home or in other hotels, so I have to figure out if 50 pounds on the hotel machine has the same resistance that it has on the one I normally use. I look for wear patterns on the weights, and I use the mark that has the most wear. That's the starting point for my workout. In the same way, we teach that our first gift sets the direction of future giving. People are often confused at this point. One person heard stories about generous gifts from people in our church, and she shook her head as she told me, "Pastor Rob, I can't give $100,000."

I assured her, "I don't expect you to, but can you give $100?"

She said, "Yeah, I can do that!"

I continued, "Just make your first Kingdom Builders gift, start working on the plan with what you can do right now, no matter how big or small, above the tithe. This sets the direction for future giving."

Jesus told us, "Wherever your treasure is, there the desires of your heart will also be" (Matthew 6:21). What you value, what drives you, what you really want determines the condition of your heart. When you start investing your money to care for the poor, the lost, the suffering, widows, orphans, and the homeless, soon your heart will be moved with compassion for them if it isn't already. You start noticing needs that didn't pop up on your radar before. As a Kingdom Builder, I'm increasingly drawn to places where poverty and the sheer mass of unbelievers must grieve God's heart, and these things are grieving mine ... places like India, Afghanistan, and China. And my heart is drawn to Ethiopia, where drought is devastating the land and the people. So the first gift above the tithe, whatever it may be, steers your heart in the direction of generosity.

When the widow put two coins in the offering at the temple, it was the equivalent of only $1.88 today, but Jesus was impressed with her heart of glad generosity and complete trust in the God who provided for her. The amount doesn't matter as much as the heart behind it. In the case of the widow in this story, her little was *all* she had! It was a small amount but a huge percentage! If your first gift doesn't seem like much, don't feel guilty, it could have been a huge percentage! Give it, knowing that it's setting the direction of your heart and that will make a difference in how you respond to God and the needs of people from that point forward. Your first gift catalyzes you to live out your *Plan*, giving what you already have in your hands. After that, it's time to ask God to give you a *vision goal*, trusting Him to provide beyond your ability. See what God does. The adventure has begun, and you'll never be the same.

Some have told me their vision goal is "to give more." I encourage them to be more specific and to ask God to give them a goal for an actual amount or a percentage. And I tell them to write it down. Writing forces us to be more precise, and it's a permanent reminder of what God has said to us. Some put it on their mirror or refrigerator to remind them to pray that God will provide, and others have it on a piece of paper in a drawer they regularly open. It doesn't matter where you have it just so you see it often enough to prod you to pray.

The progression looks like this: God takes people who are *tithing* and want to be Kingdom Builders from their *first gift* in their plan to give ... to the *next step* of their *vision goal* ... to a *big step* of their dream goal. We don't get to the dream right away—it takes time and exercise to build our giving muscles, but some people in our church are already committed to giving 90 percent of their income and live on 10 percent.

I dream of a day when Christians are so generous that God has to say, "Stop! That's enough!" Has that ever happened? Actually, yes, it has. In Exodus 35, we read about Moses telling the people, "Take a sacred offering for the Lord. Let those with generous hearts present the following gifts to the Lord." The long list includes gold and silver, the finest cloth, tanned skins, oil, spices, and gemstones. Moses then speaks to the skilled people: "Come, all of you who are gifted craftsmen. Construct everything that the Lord has commanded." This list is about the materials needed to build the Tabernacle and all the furniture that will be used in it, including the Ark's cover, the thick curtain, the lampstand, the altar, the washbasin, and everything else."

What happened? "All whose hearts were stirred and whose spirits were moved came and brought their sacred offerings to the Lord. They brought all the materials needed for the Tabernacle, for the performance of its rituals, and for the sacred garments. Both men and women came, all whose hearts were willing. They brought to the Lord their offerings of gold—brooches, earrings, rings from their fingers, and necklaces. They presented gold objects of every kind as a special offering to the Lord" (Exodus 35:5-22). The craftsmen went to work on the construction, and others used their talents to create the curtains, furniture, and items used in worship in the Tabernacle. Their hearts were really stirred!

As the days passed and work continued, the giving didn't stop: "Moses gave them the materials donated by the people of Israel as sacred offerings for the completion of the sanctuary. But the people continued to bring additional gifts each morning. Finally, the craftsmen who were working on the sanctuary left their work. They went to Moses and reported, "The people have given more than enough materials to complete the job the Lord has commanded us to do!" (Exodus 36:3-5)

What a problem! Moses sent word throughout the camp: "Men and women, don't prepare any more gifts for the sanctuary. We have enough!" (v. 6) The people weren't giving stuff out of their basements and closets that hadn't seen the light of day in years. They were giving the very best of what they had. And they weren't coldly calculating how little they could give. Their hearts were moved by the Lord to overflow with generosity!

Is anything like that possible for a church? For a ministry? I believe it is, and, in fact, our church is moving in that direction. God is creating a culture of generosity where extravagant giving is becoming the norm, not the exception. It's infectious ... in a good way! As people hear stories about others who are on the adventure, their doubts and fears begin to subside, and they find the courage to take their next steps.

Let me tell you about a few of them:

> In 2014, Ryan and Lindy experienced financial strains. As Ryan prayed, the Lord showed him that he had surrendered every area of his life to Him ... every area except one, his finances. It was a turning point for this young couple. They decided to trust God with their money. They gave faithfully for several years, and at the same time, they saved money for a down payment on

some property where they wanted to raise their three sons. But one morning in church, as they watched a video about the International Justice Mission, an organization that protects people in poverty from human trafficking, Ryan leaned over to Lindy and whispered, "I think buying the land has been our idea, not God's."

Lindy immediately agreed, "Yes, that's not how He wants us to spend our money."

Together, they decided to give the largest gift of their lives, "And we gave it with such joy," Lindy remembers. They valued kingdom impact more than personal comfort.

A few months later, the couple went on a missions trip and visited a "gospel café," where people in a largely unreached city could come to a non-threatening place to hear about Jesus. As they stood with others on the team listening to the local leader, he held his hands out and said, "All that you see here is because of Kingdom Builders at River Valley." Now, when the people who were on the team see videos and hear stories of how God is using Kingdom Builders around the world, they know their investments in these people and projects are making a difference for eternity.

Bjorn and Liz were drawn to River Valley because of their heart for missions. Bjorn's grandfather was a missionary doctor in Ethiopia, so his mother had grown up overseas involved with a cutting-edge ministry. The couple incurred substantial student loan debt, but instead of waiting until it was paid before they gave more than a tithe, they decided to do both: keep paying down their debt without missing the opportunity to give generously to missions. They were especially touched by two stories. One was about a young couple who have a coffee plantation in Asia and use their position to spread the gospel, and the other described how an elderly man had received a Bible in his own language and wept tears of joy as he held it in his hands. Bjorn reflects, "The money we give is going directly to fund ministries that are making a difference. It's an honor to play a small part in all of that. God is always moving, and He moves whether we participate with Him or not. We want to join Him."

When Iliea was six years old, her family became one of the first missionary families sent from River Valley Church. They served in Eswatini for eight years. When she returned, she was part of a giving effort in the youth group. Each student was challenged to raise $1,000 for a missions project. Iliea thought that goal was impossible, but as she prayed about it, she had the idea of starting a sweatshirt business called Iliea's Corner. After a while, she'd only sold five sweatshirts, and she was discouraged. She kept praying, and the Lord told her, "Keep trusting Me. Keep pursuing this. It'll happen if you keep going." Before long, she had $600 in sales. She needed to sell 20 more sweatshirts, and she had orders for 22. She remembers thinking, *"No way! This is so cool!"* In an interview, she explained, "You don't have to be a certain age, and you don't have to be a missionary to make a difference. You can just give, and you'll see how people benefit from your generosity. It will bring you pure joy!"

Quite often, people apologize for the size of their first gift beyond the tithe. They say, "It's just $100. I wish it could be more."

I don't hesitate: "Are you kidding? That's fantastic! I'm so excited you're on this journey with the rest of us!"

After they get a plan to give and they want to set their first vision goal, they're stepping into new territory, so they have a bit of anxiety. I tell them to relax and listen to the Lord. We tell couples to pray separately and ask God for an amount to give, and it's amazing how often they come up with the same number. It's amazing because for many couples, only one handles the money, which tends to make that person more conservative than the other. In our case, Becca is an accountant, so she doesn't let me near the bank statements—and I'm grateful she handles it all. Still, we usually hear the same message from God about how much He wants us to give. (And if a husband and wife have different numbers, I tell them the higher number must be from

> You don't have to be a certain age, and you don't have to be a missionary to make a difference. You can just give, and you'll see how people benefit from your generosity. It will bring you pure joy!

God! Just kidding. I tell them to pray again until they agree on what God has for them.) For many, being obedient to tithe is life-changing, so their first vision goal may be something like $100 a month or $1,200 for the year. If you think that wouldn't make much of a dent, let me change your perspective:

- $200 would buy the first Bible for 200 kids.
- $200 would help victims of a tornado, hurricane, fire, or another natural disaster.
- $200 would pay for resources to train a pastor in a developing country for a year.
- $200 would feed 2,000 kids for a week in an impoverished country.
- $200 would start two churches in India.
- $100 would provide evangelistic resources in a Gospel-poor country.
- $100 would allow 100 people to hear the Good News for the first time online.

Giving an additional $100 a month is enough of a stretch for a lot of individuals and couples, but again, they need to hear from God. About half of the people who set this vision goal in our church soon get ahead of this pace, so they reconfigure their goal upwards and keep getting more and more generous.

To give people a ballpark of what the muscle-building process looks like, I suggest their next *big step* is giving another five percent of their income, so a total of 15 percent, to help change the world. When those muscles become strong, it's time for a fourth step: radical generosity. Some people set a goal as a percentage of their income, probably 20 percent or more, but others have a target amount they're shooting for. Becca and I have followed this process: tithing, first planned step beyond the tithe, next step of a vision goal, the big step of the additional five percent, and radical generosity of 20 percent or more. For years, we've given more than 20 percent of our income to the church, and we couldn't be more thrilled to see God use our money to

Every choice has opportunity costs. When we choose one thing, we're saying no to something else.

accomplish incredible things locally and globally. I want you to hear me, I'm not saying this is what every person *has* to do; I'm telling you what I've lived out and seen many believers live out over my 30 years in ministry. The more we give, the larger our lives become! God has changed our hearts. When we began giving more than the tithe, it felt like a challenge, but over time as we've developed our muscle, giving is one of the most joyful things we do. We love to hear stories of how God used our last gift, and we can't wait to see how God will use the next one!

Mother Teresa once said, "I have found this paradox, that if you love until it hurts, there can be no more hurt, only more love."[16] Becca and

I want to rearrange our lives around loving God and loving the people He loves, which includes everybody. We want to alleviate suffering and bring the Gospel to people who have never heard and have no hope. Every choice has opportunity costs. When we choose one thing, we're saying no to something else. If Becca and I spend a lot of money on things that don't matter for eternity, we won't have it to invest in advancing the kingdom. But we've made a different choice: we want everything about us, including how we use the money God has put in our hands, to love people in Jesus' name. We began years ago with the tithe, advanced to a first planned gift above it, made the shift to the next step of another five percent, and graduated to 20 percent and beyond, and then experienced the thrill of radical generosity. We didn't begin with the big step of 20 percent, but we got there, and we feel enormously blessed to be God's partner in sharing the message of Christ and caring for the needy in our neighborhoods and all around the world.

At a local event, I met a CPA who prepares taxes for a wide range of people, mostly those of significant wealth. I asked, "How many tax returns do you see where people tithe?"

He said, "I can probably count them on both hands. Actually, it's so few that I could name the people."

"Then how many give 20 percent?"

He almost laughed as he said, "Are you kidding me? That's for people with foundations and legacy wealth."

"Not really," I said. "It's for people who know they're blessed by God and want to be a blessing to others." He still wasn't buying it.

Yet of the people in our church, about 40 percent are giving above their tithe to Kingdom Builders. Here's the breakdown of our Kingdom Builders giving:

- 68% gave less than $1,000.
- 23% gave between $1,000 and $4,999.
- 7% gave between $5,000 and $24,999.
- 1% gave between $25,000 and $100,000.
- 0.2% gave over $100,000.

As you can see from this breakdown, God uses regular people working together to do amazing things. With everyone doing their part, in 2023, our church was able to give away over $10 million to projects in our community and around the world.

I can't tell you how many times I've thanked people for being so generous to Kingdom Builders, and with tears running down their faces, they say, "No, Pastor Rob. Thank YOU! This is the most exciting thing I've ever been involved in." But let me be honest: other people have left our church and have said, "I just don't feel comfortable at River Valley. You have such an emphasis on missions and giving generously to change the world. I'm not that interested in what you're doing. You're trying to do too much. We can't be so focused on the world." Which always makes me sad because Jesus said, "To whom much is given much is required." And when I travel the globe, I realize the church I pastor has been given much and so much is required.

I don't believe we're out of balance at all. Eighty percent of the wealth in the hands of Christians on planet Earth is in America, but 42 percent of the eight billion people in the world have never heard a clear presentation of the gospel of Jesus Christ. Only one percent of money given for global missions is designated to reach unreached people groups.[17] God has given the American church the resources to make a huge dent in fulfilling the Great Commission (to go into all the world and preach the

Good News of God's forgiveness), and in fact, we have a solemn responsibility to be good stewards who have God's heart for all people and do all we can to be His partners in changing lives. We're not asking anyone to do anything they don't want to do. We want to invite people to take God's hand and join Him in the greatest adventure and the greatest enterprise the world has ever known. Will that involve sacrifice? Absolutely. Will it call out the very best in us? You bet. Is it worth it? *One hundred percent yes!*

Eighty percent of the wealth in the hands of Christians on planet Earth is in America, but 42 percent of the eight billion people in the world have never heard a clear presentation of the gospel of Jesus Christ.

I asked a man who has given generously to Kingdom Builders what motivates him to give so much. He told me, "My wife and I are giving 50 percent of our income. We continue to be humbled by what God is doing through us. We've never had the mindset of 'give to get,' but we see God's blessings over and over. We continue to set dream goals without knowing where it will come from, but God always shows up. Some would call it 'radical giving,' but I call it 'confident giving'—confidence in Him."

At River Valley, we aren't on the lookout to see what kind of cars people drive, what kind of houses they live in, or where they go on vacations. We don't have someone in a secluded office formulating some kind of metric to run the numbers so we can tell people what they should give above their tithe. It's entirely between them and God. Whatever He puts on their hearts, whatever they can cheerfully give, they should give. Nothing more, nothing less.

When we make our ask for the annual Miracle Offering (the day we give our biggest and best financial gift to complete all the projects on our list), I make sure people have an out. I tell them, "If you don't want to participate with us, if you feel pressured, or maybe you're even angry we are doing this today, I want you to write one word on your contribution envelope: 'Why?' You're asking, 'Why would these people give generously, joyfully, and willingly to spread the message of Jesus?' I pray that God will answer your prayer and give you the 'why.'" Quite often, He does … and it's a beautiful thing. And when people really want to give but can't at that moment, I tell them, "Write 'Next year' on your envelope, and keep the goal in front of you until you give it. When you do, watch to see how strong you will become in giving. You'll be thrilled when it finally happens, and you'll have no doubt that giving *is* a muscle!"

chapter seven

Meaning to Your Money

A few years ago, a local newspaper ran an article about how much the people of River Valley Church give. The article was very positive, but the online comments? Not so much. Many of the people were obviously angry. One represented several others: "Your priorities are wrong. How can you give so much to needs overseas when we have big needs here? The money should have been given to care for our people." Some people were critical of how we used the money, but no one condemned how much we gave. The article and the comments caused quite a stir in our church. I reminded our people, "We don't charge dues at River Valley. We don't require a certain level of giving to come to our church. No one is promised Heaven if they give this amount or that percentage. It's all about responding to God's grace poured out in Jesus." I let that sink in, and then I explained, "The reason they're upset is that we don't love their god like they do. Their god is money—and the possessions and power and pleasure it can buy. We don't respect their god, and that's what infuriates them. We have a different God, and we're using the money God has entrusted us with to fulfill His mission."

Jesus taught, "No one can serve two masters; for either he will hate the one and love the other, or else he will be loyal to the one and despise the other. You cannot serve God and mammon" (Matthew 6:24 NKJV). Many translations use "wealth" in place of mammon, but that's a bit misleading. *Mammon* is a Chaldee or Syriac word that personifies riches, so it means "the god of riches."[18] We love and serve whatever we value supremely. If it's money, our lives revolve around it, and we make decisions based on our ability to acquire and use it. Money becomes the way we define meaning and purpose, and it's the natural bent of the fallen human heart. Let me be clear: Money isn't the problem; it's our devotion to money that's a huge problem. Paul explained this point to Timothy: "For the love of money is the root of all kinds of evil. And some people, craving money, have wandered from the true faith and pierced themselves with many sorrows" (1 Timothy 6:10). We don't overcome our love and devotion to this god very easily. It takes something else, something more attractive and powerful to replace it.

Let me warn you, criticism will come. When you declare you are going to live a generous life, people (most of whom give little to nothing, by the way) will criticize you for every purchase you make. We've had people make videos and social media posts about our family. Someone reading this now needs this lesson, you can't please the critics! Generosity isn't about perfection; it's about being responsive to what God is asking you to do. Material possessions aren't all bad, having a nice home isn't sinful. You aren't angering God by enjoying the vacation that you earned. I love what my friend George Kamel says, "Skymiles won't

keep you from going to heaven, they just aren't worth anything there."
Two hundred years ago, Scottish pastor Thomas Chalmers wrote an essay
that describes how Christians can change, or more accurately, how God
changes us. He observed that our preferences won't change by realizing
they exist and despising ourselves for having them. ("I'm such a terrible
person for focusing on money. I have to stop!") And they won't cease
to exist if we pretend they're not there. ("Hey, no problem with money
here.") We can't simply and easily give up the gods that have captured our
hearts for so long. Another, more powerful solution is needed. Chalmers
explained, "The only way to dispossess [the heart] of an old affection is by
the expulsive power of a new one."[19] When our love for God is stronger,
more attractive, more life-giving than the god of riches, wealth ceases
to hold the position of god in our hearts. It becomes a tool we can use to
honor the One who has taken its place.

So ... what's the difference between money being our god or just a
tool we can use to honor God? How can we tell if mammon still has us
in its grip? When I go to the doctor, he uses several measurements to
determine if I'm healthy: weight, temperature, blood pressure, heart rate,
EKG, and blood tests. These tests give a clear indication of my health.
In the same way, we can use ever-improving financial apps to see how
much money came in, how much we spent, how much we saved, and
how much we gave. These amounts (or percentages) are a very good
indication of the health of our hearts. Beyond the raw numbers, we can
analyze our daydreams and nightmares: what do we think about when
we have nothing pressing?

Do we imagine a kitchen redo, getting a new car, or going on an
expensive vacation? Or do our minds drift toward caring for people in
need and being part of the solution for them?

What stories do we tell others? Do we talk mostly about our acquisitions, pleasures, and conquests, or do we tell stories about God doing amazing things in and through us?

And are our hearts moved when we watch the news and see images of people devastated by famine, war, or terrorism? Several years ago, singer Jack Johnson released "The News," a song that describes a mother's attempts to protect her child from the harsh realities shown in newscasts. She tries to tell her child that the deaths and destruction they see are just make-believe, but she realizes something is missing from the telecast. She asks:

"Why don't the newscasters cry when they read about the people who die?

You'd think they could be decent enough to put just a tear in their eyes."[20]

Are we "decent enough" to cry when we read about or see pictures of young children who don't have clean water or enough food, families torn apart by conflict, or bodies broken and lives lost in disasters? These images are the stock-in-trade of mainstream and cable news, but it's easy to become anesthetized and numb to them because we're exposed to them so often. Do we get more upset that someone dinged our paint job with their car door, that a neighbor has a bigger boat, or that no one noticed our haircut or new clothes?

Jay Bennett is a friend who is the Chairman of the Board of the National Christian Foundation, an organization that distributes billions of dollars to worthy causes. He explains that tithing and generosity are forms of worship, ways that we deepen our intimacy with God. He uses a creative illustration to demonstrate the power of the spirit of mammon. I asked if I could use it at River Valley, and he was glad for me to. I had someone come on stage with a roll of Saran Wrap and begin to wrap it around me. I explained, "Mammon, the desire for more and more stuff, is like this clear wrap. We don't even notice it. Before long, we're trapped, but we aren't sure why. We want to be free to use our money for the Lord, but we can't. Mammon tells us lies—like we can't let go of our hard-earned money, we need it to feel secure, and we deserve every penny. Besides, we want more stuff. Our financial and spiritual arms are bound up, and our reach is limited. How is the spirit of mammon broken? When we begin to tithe, one arm is freed, and when we begin to give above the tithe, the other arm is freed. Mammon loses its grip on us." As the clear wrap dropped to my feet on stage, I continued, "But mammon is always nearby. It runs to wrap us when we're at the mall, in the golf pro shop, in the game store, when we're scrolling through stuff we want online, and where anything else is sold. Mammon will be near us for the rest of our lives, but it doesn't have to keep us captive. We can be free by choosing to follow God in tithing and generosity."

Do you want to be free from mammon? I know you do. That's why you're reading this book. If you'd like to watch the sermon I'm referencing, you can scan the QR code.

Now, there's something we need to address. It's debt. Fewer than one in four American households is debt-free, and the rest have some form of consumer debt, averaging about $38,000, not including a mortgage on their homes.[21] This means that a lot of people who are reading this book feel pulled in opposite directions—they want to give more, but they need to pay off their consumer debt.

About 20 years ago, a couple moved to our area from Tennessee, and I noticed they gave very generously to the church. One day, I asked the husband about it, and he told me their story. He said, "I had to have a fast car, so I bought a Corvette. It was a thrill … for a little while. Then, I didn't own it; it owned me. I was a slave to the lender until Dave Ramsey taught us how to manage money. My wife and I sold a lot of stuff we didn't need, and we paid down our debt until it was all gone. We've been debt-free since then, and we can give more to the Lord. The only thing we pay on now is our house payment." Then he had an idea. "Pastor Rob, would you like me to teach *Financial Peace University* at River Valley?"

"Yes, I would!" I replied in an instant. Since then, thousands of families in our church have participated in a *Financial Peace* group, and we now resource more people with Dave's digital financial tool, *Ramsey+*, than any church in the nation. It has helped thousands of people get out of debt and live more generously. Who would have thought the guy who started his church on $100,000 in credit cards would be helping thousands get out of debt? Only God!

At one point early in our marriage, Becca and I owed about $4,000 in credit card debt, and we were making the minimum payment each month (which means we would have it paid off sometime before retirement). We'd taken a vacation and charged everything, knowing we didn't have enough money to pay it off when the bill came. And then Becca's grandmother died, leaving us $5,000. We gave a tithe of $500 and then we paid off our debt. We made a commitment to never get "underwater" again and use credit cards to live above our means. That was more than 25 years ago, and thankfully, we've kept that commitment. We've lived within our means, we've paid cash, and escaped the trap of consumer debt.

The Bible doesn't say you are sinning for borrowing money. Most Christian financial experts teach that a reasonable mortgage on a house is acceptable because it's an appreciating asset. The stuff we buy on credit cards doesn't appreciate! But the Scriptures warn that borrowing is risky. We become enslaved to the lender (Proverbs 22:7), and it must be completely paid back (Exodus 22:14). Author and speaker Randy Alcorn asks some piercing questions many of us need to think about:

- Is the obligation of repayment worth the value you receive? The new smell wears off pretty fast.
- Is not having enough to pay for the item or service God's way of saying "not now" or "no"?
- What is the message we're sending to God that we need more than He has provided for us?
- Will today's debt hinder tomorrow's freedom? We have to help a lot of people who want to be missionaries get out of debt so they can go.
- Are we mortgaging the future for today's whims?
- Is it really a need, or is it a want? Paul told the Philippians about God's promise: "And this same God who takes care of me will supply all your needs from his glorious riches, which have been given to us in Christ Jesus" (Philippians 4:19).[22]

Debt hangs over us like a dark cloud … or maybe like a vicious monster. It haunts our thoughts, oppresses our hearts, creates conflict in our marriages and with our kids, and erodes our confidence. Like an addict, we become less than truthful about the scale of the problem. We insist, "I'm fine. No problem. Nothing to see here." For many people in debt, when they get a raise or a windfall like a bonus, instead of using the money to pay down the money they owe, they raise their standard of living and their standard of borrowing, and they get even deeper in debt. A better strategy is that when we get a raise or some unexpected money, we tithe on it, pay off debt, and put the rest in the bank. When we get another raise or a surprise windfall, we can start living into the previous raise and tithe and save the new one. (I wish I'd learned that a long time ago!)

People have asked me, "How much should I leave my kids?" It's not a simple question to answer. David Green, the owner of Hobby Lobby, commented, "If we pass only money to the next generation, we lay a crushing load upon them. The inheritance of greater value is the sum of how we live, what we believe, and the content of the dreams that carry us to success."[23] Similarly, Randy Alcorn advises, "We should not transfer wealth to adult children unless we've successfully transferred wisdom to them."[24] I remember a conversation I had with my mom and siblings. She told us about her financial situation, and she wondered how she should leave her assets to us. We told her, "Mom, spend it all! You and Dad gave us so much more than money. You've given us faith in Jesus Christ, confidence that we could follow Him wherever He leads, a loving home, and the ability to hear God's voice. You've blessed us in so many ways." I hope Connor and Logan will say the same things to Becca and me someday.

Consumer debt can be a problem for people who make $30,000 a year and for those who make $3 million a year. Oscar winner Nicholas Cage admitted that he blew through his $150 million fortune and was $6 million in debt to the IRS. He had bought lavish homes all over the world, and then the real estate market crashed. He took "crummy" roles to make enough money to pay back what he owed.[25]

At our church, we've had two couples who got deep in debt even though they made $250,000 a year. They asked us for benevolence, but instead, we paid for them to attend *Financial Peace University*. I explained to one of the couples, "You need to sell things you don't need, including things you really like, and live on simple dinners until you've paid everything off. If you're disciplined and determined, it won't take as long as you think." They looked at me like I'd just stepped out of an alien craft from a distant galaxy.

The husband finally said, "Can't you help us get back where we were?"

"No," I told him. "This is a reset, not a redo."

A man who lost his job asked the church for benevolence. When helping him go over his finances, we discovered he had almost a million dollars in his retirement account. We told him the purpose of our benevolence fund isn't to give to millionaires, but he insisted, "But if I take any of that money out, I'll incur a penalty."

"Yes," we responded. "But you'll still have almost a million dollars in the account!" He didn't see the logic in our argument. This doesn't mean the church only helps people who do everything right but rather a lesson that you can't outearn your financial decisions.

One day, my son Logan told me, "Dad, it's great that we have the opportunity to add meaning to people's money." I knew there was more to his thinking than this one line, so I waited for him to explain. "They could use all their money for things that don't count for eternity, but if they're living for God, He gives meaning to their money. Then, their motivation for making more money isn't to spend it on themselves but to have a greater impact for the kingdom."

Instantly, I realized he was on to something. I began asking people questions to help them connect meaning to their money. The first one is: "What act of generosity gives you the most fulfillment?"

Many have to think for a few seconds and then say something like, "Sponsoring a child" or "Funding an orphanage" or "The time we gave for flood victims in Florida."

I then ask, "Besides your house, what's the biggest purchase you've ever made?"

I don't have to wait for the answers to this question. Immediately, they talk about their boat or car or property on a lake.

I ask, "Do you know your ABT?"

Of course, they look at me like I'm speaking in some obscure computer coding language, so I tell them, "It's your 'accumulated blessing total.' It's the kingdom impact you've had with your money over your lifetime."

They try to do a quick calculation in their heads before they say anything, but I can tell that most of them are stumped. It's not a concept they've come across before. In the language of this book, it's the impact of their tithe, plan, vision, and dream. Becca and I keep track of the projects we've donated to so we can put pictures of people with the numbers in our tally, and we keep a running total of all we give toward our ultimate dream goal.

Next, I ask, "What's the incredible next thing God has for you?" I usually need to paint a clearer picture: "What do you sense God is asking you to do to partner with Him?"

And then I ask the grand final question: "What's your future impossible dream goal that only God can accomplish?"

I always conduct these conversations in private: at dinner, playing golf, on missions trips, and at other times when I want to impart the principles about money that God has given me. People who are just starting the journey of generosity have a lot of questions about the first steps, and those who are well along the path have questions about how they can maximize their impact. All the conversations are rich and meaningful … just as I hoped and planned. They also pull people up to a higher way of living and keep the spirit of mammon at bay.

I get so excited to see how God uses the concepts of plan-vision-dream to capture the hearts of the givers and accomplish incredible things for Christ around the world that I have no hesitation inviting others to join us. Not a shred of guilt, not a bit of pressure … just the joy of trusting God to do amazing things and see Him come through time after time.

When one of our couples gave the church our first gift of $1 million, I was thrilled, amazed, and overwhelmed with what God had entrusted our church with. As I thanked God, I sensed Him ask, "How many families in your church do you want to see give $1 million?"

Instantly, I said, "Fifty." (I probably should have said a thousand, but fifty seemed plenty big to me.) It was at that moment that I felt permission to ask other people to go on this incredible generosity journey to do so much good.

I started meeting with wealthy people in our church who had generous hearts, and I asked them to pray about giving $1 million over and above their tithe. I didn't put a deadline on them, and I didn't have any idea how God might provide. I only asked them to pray and ask if giving $1 million beyond the tithe is a dream goal God might give them and if they would do it as fast as the Lord provided it for them.

What I'm inviting these people to do really has less to do with money than with discovering the joy of using their gifts for God. I saw this clearly demonstrated at our church in a case that had nothing to do with money. Two young women were working in our church café serving donuts and coffee … and then someone happened to see them singing in a YouTube video. Turns out they're fantastic singers! We asked them to use their singing gift, and now they're part of the worship team at the church.

It's the same thing I'm trying to do with couples and individuals who have the skill set and ability of making money—encouraging them to use that gift for God to reach more people with the gospel. Almost all of them have had tears in their eyes as they said, "Yes, count me in. I want my money to have meaning in the kingdom." In one conversation, the wife wept with joyful anticipation of God using them in such a big way. Through her tears, she told me, "Pastor, we don't need another house, another boat, or another car. I'd much rather build churches around the world."

A few people have told me, "Pastor, I think you're overestimating me. I'm already at my limit."

I respond, "That's great! Keep doing what you're doing. I'm so grateful for you." Generosity is the point, not the dollar amount.

Only a couple of people weren't excited about the possibility. One said, "No, that's not me. I don't want to live like that." One of them was already giving a lot to the church, but he didn't have a vision for more. I simply thanked him for giving so much already. I'm not trying to pressure people into giving more. I'm trying to give meaning to their money.

You may be thinking, "Your church must have a lot of really rich people." Actually, I don't think the demographics of our church are much different from most others. One study found there are 5.3 million millionaires and 770 billionaires in America. Millionaires make up about two percent of the adult population[26], so I think it's safe to conclude that many churches have at least one and probably more than one.

I call the ones who catch the vision of giving $1 million "B3s," which stands for Blessed to Be a Blessing. Quite often, when I have the conversation to share my vision and ask them to pray about joining us, God has already been working in their hearts to make them receptive and eager. I played golf with a couple of guys who attend our church, but I wasn't planning on talking to them about anything specific. I was just expecting a day of golf with guys from our church. Yet, on the second hole, one of them asked me, "Pastor Rob, is there anything going on with Kingdom Builders that you're excited about?"

I could have talked for an hour, but I just shared a few projects that touched my heart. Every couple of holes, he asked another question about projects, trips, and generosity. When we finished the round, the three of us had lunch. It took a while for the Holy Spirit to convince me that this was the time to talk to him about it (I can be pretty slow!), but I told him, "I wasn't going to talk about this today, but it seems you're really interested in Kingdom Builders. I'm talking to a few people to ask them to pray and ask God if He wants them to give $1 million as soon as they can. Would you possibly be one of those people?"

> To give meaning to our money, we need to connect the dots, pay attention to where the money is going, and especially be aware of the impact of our money on real people—around the corner and around the world.

His eyes lit up. "Yes! I'm in!"

I was stunned. I asked, "How could you say yes so fast?"

He smiled and told me, "This morning as I was praying, I sensed the Lord tell me to bring my checkbook to the golf course today. All day, I thought you might ask me to pay for a project, but you've asked me to go on the journey of a lifetime!"

I looked at the other guy at the table and wondered how he was processing this conversation. I told him, "Hey, no pressure."

He tilted his head and grinned. "You can't pressure me. I'm a business owner. I'm in, too."

On the way home, I got a text from the man who had asked so many questions all day. He wrote that only seconds after we left, he got a report from his team about an increase in sales and the upward projections of future revenues. He wrote, "I find it more than coincidental that God was working on me and my company at the same time."

After the services at one of our church locations, a young couple came up to talk to me. The husband asked, "Pastor, is there anything in the church that provides mentoring for people who want to give more?"

> Don't do the math; just do your part. When everyone does what God asks them to do, there's always more than enough.

For some reason, I sensed God leading me to bypass his question. Instead, I asked, "Has God given you a number, an amount you're supposed to give?"

He and his wife looked at each other, looked back at me, and then at each other again. She almost whispered to him, "Can we say this number out loud?"

I interrupted, "It's a million dollars, isn't it?"

They looked shocked and said in unison, "Yes!"

"I've been praying for you."

Both of them started crying. He asked, "What do you mean?"

I explained, "I've been praying that God would send us 50 families who will give $1 million over their tithe as soon as the Lord provides it."

"We're one of them," he stated emphatically. "That's the way we want to live."

Of course, the vast majority of people in our church (and every other church) don't have the capacity to give a million dollars. The point of this chapter is to connect giving to something far more rewarding than writing a check or doing a monthly transfer and not thinking about what it accomplishes. To give meaning to our money, we need to connect the dots, pay attention to where the money is going, and especially be aware of the impact of our money on real people—around the corner and around the world.

> **God wants to work His love so deeply in your heart that it expels every lesser god. When that happens, you become generous.**

The lie of the enemy is, "Your gift doesn't matter." That's simply not true. Every gift counts, both for the impact on the people served and for the giver who receives the "Well done" from the Father. At our church, generosity for most of us is modest, but so many are giving just above the tithe that it accumulates for a powerful kingdom impact. Don't do the math; just do your part. When everyone does what God asks them to do, there's always more than enough.

Some of you have been around a while, and you want your remaining years to matter. You give because you want to leave a legacy of generosity to your kids and grandkids.

Some of you are in productive years when you're making the most money, and it's easy to make pleasure, possessions, and positions your god. God wants to work His love so deeply in your heart that it expels every lesser god. When that happens, you become generous.

And some of you are young. You aren't making much money yet, but God is tugging on your heart. It's wise to set the trajectory of wise and generous money management now before bad habits and bad decisions derail your God-inspired goals.

All of us can celebrate the generosity we see in others. No matter who we are and how much we give, we can be thrilled that God is changing hearts, giving each of us the desire to use our money in ways that make a difference. We are all in this together. Those of limited means give generously, and those who can give far more are no more generous. This isn't a competition, so there's no room for boasting or jealousy. It's all about Him and His kingdom, not being one-up on someone else. We're on the same journey and on the same team.

God is just as thrilled with your generosity if you do what He whispers to you as He is with someone who gives $1 million. At one of our smaller campuses (we are a multi-site church with over a dozen locations), I shared how God had impressed people to give millions to Kingdom Builders across our campuses. That campus had given about $100,000 total for the year, and I could see discouraged faces in the room. It was like they were collectively telling me, "Pastor, what did our giving matter? It was so small compared to everyone else's."

At that moment, I stopped the service and told them, "Listen, God just wanted you to be obedient, and He's thrilled with your response to His leading. He didn't ask you to give millions. He only asked you to pray, listen, and follow Him. I celebrate your obedience to God."

We need God's perspective on what's important. Two things will last for eternity: people and God's Word. Everything else will come to an end. God has a plan for the biggest bonfire the world has ever known. Peter warns us, "But the day of the Lord will come like a thief. The heavens will disappear with a roar; the elements will be destroyed by fire, and the earth and everything done in it will be laid bare" (2 Peter 3:10 NIV). When I taught this truth at a men's retreat, I told them, "Guys, your boat is going to burn. God is okay with you having it, but just know that it's going up in flames. The people you reach and influence for Christ, that's what lasts." I could tell they were thinking hard about what I said, so I pressed a little more: "Some of you are hesitant to tithe. How can you trust Jesus for your eternity, but you don't want Him to touch your heart enough so you can let go of ten percent and live on a mission with God?"

Far too often, we live segmented lives: We sing about God's greatness and grace in church, but we don't let our worship filter down into what makes every aspect of our lives meaningful. Be consistent. Give God your heart, give Him your worship, give Him your time and talents, and let Him lead you to manage your money with a kingdom perspective. When you do, you'll see how much difference it makes when you give meaning to your money.

chapter eight

Ride the Wave

As King David prepared to depart from the scene and turn the kingdom over to his son Solomon, he knew that Solomon was going to build the Temple in Jerusalem, a permanent building to replace the portable Tabernacle. The construction of the Temple had to honor God, so nothing would be spared. Out of his own treasury, he gave 112 tons of gold and 262 tons of silver to coat the walls. After he announced his contribution, he told the leaders of the nation, "Now then, who will follow my example and give offerings to the LORD today?" (1 Chronicles 29:5)

> Then the family leaders, the leaders of the tribes of Israel, the generals and captains of the army, and the king's administrative officers all gave willingly. For the construction of the Temple of God, they gave about 188 tons of gold, 10,000 gold coins, 375 tons of silver, 675 tons of bronze, and 3,750 tons of iron. They also

> contributed numerous precious stones, which were deposited in the treasury of the house of the LORD under the care of Jehiel, a descendant of Gershon. The people rejoiced over the offerings, for they had given freely and wholeheartedly to the LORD, and King David was filled with joy. (vv. 6-9)

The progression is important: David gave generously first, then the leaders were motivated to give in the same generous spirit, and then the people joined in to give "freely and wholeheartedly." David led them in a joyous praise to God for His faithfulness throughout the generations, and the next day, the people "brought 1,000 bulls, 1,000 rams, and 1,000 male lambs as burnt offerings to the Lord. They also brought liquid offerings and many other sacrifices on behalf of all (of) Israel. They feasted and drank in the Lord's presence with great joy that day" (vv. 21-22).

Author Simon Sinek famously stated, "Leaders eat last," but in the world of generosity, leaders give first.

At River Valley, we follow this model. Much of the giving is done in the last part of the year, and we want to ride the wave of eager generosity. We start this wave in October at a banquet with hundreds of people and most of our leaders. We share our vision again, tell inspiring stories about how God has used their giving in the past, and point to our goal for the end of the year. I believe when leaders get excited to give, the whole church gets excited. We let them know that as leaders, they will create this wave starting with the offering at this banquet, and we make the ask right there. Following this banquet in November, we have our "Miracle Offering" weekend. We update what our church has done so far and ask once again for the entire church to join us in generous giving. In December, we keep people informed that the gap between commitments and actual giving is closing, and we celebrate God's faithfulness in and through our people. Actually, each year we have a number of "gap closers," people who ask, "What projects aren't fully funded? I'll give what's needed."

For the first nine months of the year, we have our regular giving rhythms of tithing and generosity beyond the tithe as we ask, update, celebrate, and rest every month. (I usually do a three-part series on finances every February, so this is very familiar to our congregation. Also, I have learned over time to see all the good that happens when people live generously, and I approach this with excitement!) In the final three months, our banquet with leaders creates a wave of generosity. Our people ride that wave at the Miracle Offering, and we ride together all the way to the beach on December 31. I'm grateful for those who take their first step and next step in January and join the adventure of generosity, and I'm grateful for those who give so much to close the gap at the end of the year. We're all in it together.

As any leader knows, momentum isn't something you can take for granted, and when you have it, you sure don't want to waste it. We build momentum monthly in our regular rhythm, and we give it an extra shot of adrenaline in the last three months. I can almost feel the anticipation grow as our entire church gets increasingly excited about hitting our goals and having a greater impact for Jesus. Let me tell just a couple of stories about couples who had very different views of money.

Calvin and Michaela's hearts have been captured by the vision to help people. Michaela remembers that in the early years of their marriage, "Calvin and I couldn't have been more different in how we handled finances. Calvin was a free spirit. He spent money on anything and everything." He was sure more money was coming in, so he didn't worry about spending what was in the bank. But Michaela was afraid of not having enough, so she was hesitant to let any go out of their account for paying bills, giving, or anything else. It's not a surprise that the difference caused a strain in their relationship. She continued, "One day we realized we were $100,000 in debt. When we heard about Kingdom Builders projects, we wanted to give, but a lot had to change if we were going to get where we wanted to be with our finances."

The couple had never created a budget, so they had no boundaries on their spending. Calvin started listening to the Dave Ramsey podcast, and together, they created their first budget. Michaela remembers, "The math showed that we'd be debt-free in two-and-a-half years. It took a few months for us to get into our groove, but then we cut back on a lot of expenses: groceries, gas, vacations, eating out, and things like that." Finances had caused a lot of pain for them, but now it was a source of healing in their relationship. They didn't cut back on tithing, and they found ways to give to Kingdom Builders projects.

The next November, when the church had the annual Miracle Offering, Calvin asked God for direction, and He gave Calvin a number … a large number. When he told Michaela, she responded, "Let's do it!" (Let me say it again: We ask people to pray and listen, and then do what God says. No one from the church interjects. It's between the person or couple and God.) Calvin's and Michaela's tenacity to cut expenses had a positive impact on their debt reduction timeline, and they determined to be debt-free by the next Miracle Offering. They encouraged each other (and themselves) by posting statements and verses around their house. They gave more than they ever dreamed possible and felt the joy of living blessed to be a blessing.

Calvin reflected, "That was really the goal of all the changes we were making with our spending—to be more generous. When we were able to give our part of the Miracle Offering, it felt surreal. We were honored to do it."

Michaela jumped in, "Calvin and I are happier than we've ever been. It's amazing, and it's only the beginning of what the Lord has for us."

When Sam and Rachel got married, they quickly realized they were living on opposite poles of the financial globe. Sam loves spreadsheets. He's a saver and a cautious spender. Rachel just hoped the checking account was above zero at the end of the month. Rachel's dad talked to Sam about Sam's journey to be debt-free, and he asked how Sam and Rachel were doing. Sam was honest about their student loan debt, money owed on their credit cards, and two car payments. His father-in-law wasn't condemning. He said simply, "Sam, you're just normal." But that word lit a fire in Sam! He wanted to be anything but normal. He began crafting a plan to get out of debt so they'd have more money to give, and he wanted to present his plan very clearly to Rachel. He'd hoped for a low-key conversation, but, he says, "Instead, it was a word vomit." Rachel didn't want to change her spending habits, yet gradually, she saw the benefits of saving, paying off debt, and being free to give more. They created a budget to guide their spending, and in eight months, they paid every penny they owed.

Rachel remembers the night when they made their last payment. They both looked at the computer screen at the transfer, and they hit "send" together. That moment changed their lives. Rachel remarked, "When we were in debt, we focused on the money we owed all the time. It was a weight on us. But now we're looking forward. There's literally nothing holding us back."

Freedom enabled them to respond more quickly to the Lord's leading. Sam shared a pivotal moment: "I sensed the Lord say, 'I've ingrained generosity in you. It's woven into your heart. You couldn't see it before, but you can now.'" Sam and Rachel created their own fund so when they hear about a need in the community, they can meet it in an instant. They call it "the generosity fund. The passage in Proverbs, "The borrower is slave to the lender" was an accurate and painful description of them before they were debt-free, but it no longer defines them.

I've noticed that kids often lead their families in generosity. When they catch the vision of using their resources to reach the lost and care for the hurting, they intuitively challenge their parents to join them. But I've seen some parents squash their kids' generous hearts! They ask, "Johnny, are you sure you want to give that much? You want that new video game, don't you? If you give that much, you won't be able to afford it." Or they say, "Don't give all your birthday money to the orphanage. Give five dollars and keep the rest." I'm afraid that these parents are actively training their kids to follow mammon instead of God. Does that sound harsh? I'm just sharing what I have seen in families over and over again. I saw it with our own sons and taught them to be generous and celebrated their generous giving. I even joked to my wife, Becca, "They have no bills, so what a great time to learn generosity!"

The kids at our church are incredibly generous. Our staff members who work with them do a fantastic job of sharing the vision of big-hearted giving. A six-year-old boy came home from church one day and told his dad, "I think we should rob a bank."

His father was more than a little surprised that this would be the lesson his son learned in church that morning. He told him, "Son, we're not going to rob a bank. It's not our money. Why do you want to do that anyway?"

The boy replied, "Because that's where the money is." (Move over, Jesse James!) "We could get that money and give it all away to missionaries."

When the dad told me about this interchange, he laughed and said, "Pastor, obviously I have a lot of discipling left to do with my son! But as his dad, I was thrilled to see his heart for God and the kingdom!"

Let me give parents a few suggestions to encourage their kids to be generous:

- Invite your kids to pray, ask God for a plan, a vision, and a dream, and obey what He tells them. When I was in junior high, I wanted to go to a movie. When I asked my parents if I could go, they told me to pray about it and do what God told me to do. When I prayed, I sensed God didn't want me to go. Going or not going wasn't the main point. It was that my parents wanted me to learn to hear the voice of God and develop a responsive heart. It was a gift they gave me that has been priceless.

- Be open with your kids about your process of identifying your plan, vision, and dream. You don't have to tell them the amount you give, but let them see behind the curtain so they get a glimpse of how God is giving you a more generous heart.

- Let your kids put your Kingdom Builders check in the offering or press "Send" for an online transfer. My suggestion would be not to do this with your tithe because they'll do the math and know how much income you earn, which may be best kept private for now. But it can be a great lesson with your Kingdom Builders contribution. When a man on our staff team was a boy sitting in church with his parents, they gave him the check and asked him to put it in the offering. The number was larger than anything he'd ever imagined, and it revolutionized his concept of generosity. Now, this young man is on our pastoral staff and is living a life of generosity that keeps on growing and growing.

- Take your kids on a trip—to a local ministry or a foreign land—so they see the impact of the family's contribution. Words at home may be descriptive, but putting them face to face with people in need is far more powerful. And as they join others on these trips, they realize they're riding a wave like everyone else. I've challenged our church to save up for this just like most families do with Disney World. We save, sacrifice, and scrimp to show them "It's a Small World." Why not do the same to show them God's big world? It will change their lives for sure.

- As a family, pray for the mission project of the month. If your church doesn't have one, keep a stack of cards with information about organizations and projects your church supports, and pray regularly for them. Just one minute at dinner can set your child's generous heart on fire.

- Take your kids with you to the store to buy groceries, clothes, school supplies, Christmas presents, and anything else the church's benevolence ministry is providing. When Connor and Logan were boys, I took them with me to the grocery store and told them, "We're filling this basket with food for people who don't have enough. Will you help me pick stuff out for them?" They were all in—and they picked the good stuff. One Christmas, Becca and I took the boys to a large store and told them, "We're buying presents for Christmas, and we want you to pick out what you like. We're giving each of you $50." They were so excited. They were very selective and wanted to get the most for their money. When we went to check out, they paid for the items, and we told them, "These aren't for your Christmas presents. They're for kids who won't have presents unless someone buys them some. We weren't sure what kids your age would like, so we trusted you to pick out really good stuff." After they got over their initial disappointment, they were glad they'd played a role in giving gifts kids really wanted. (But Becca and I were paying attention and went back later to get our boys some of the things they liked.)

- When we have missionaries or leaders of organizations speak at our church, we ask them to speak to our kids and the youth group, too. When parents know their kids have heard what they've heard, they can talk about it after the service and reinforce the needs they heard about and saw on the videos. It's also a lot of fun to let kids ask questions of the missionaries and then pray for them.

Some people believe they shouldn't talk about their giving, not even to their children. Such suggestions make them uneasy. They cite Jesus when He preached, "Watch out! Don't do your good deeds publicly, to be admired by others, for you will lose the reward from your Father in Heaven. When you give to someone in need, don't do as the hypocrites do—blowing trumpets in the synagogues and streets to call attention to their acts of charity! I tell you the truth, they have received all the reward they will ever get. But when you give to someone in need, don't let your left hand know what your right hand is doing. Give your gifts in private, and your Father, who sees everything, will reward you" (Matthew 6:1-4).

A trumpet was a musical instrument, though not much like the modern version you may be familiar with. But Jesus may have been referring to another way to "blow your own horn." Offerings in the temple were collected in large, trumpet-shaped metal containers. People could drop their coins in carefully so they didn't make noise, or they could blast them into the trumpet, making a racket and seeing how many heads they could turn to call attention to their gift. That's exactly what Jesus warned against: doing "your good deeds publicly, to be admired by others." He's addressing the motivation for letting people know what we're giving. As we saw, David was very descriptive about his offering for the construction of the Temple, and he was careful to list all the contributions of the leaders and the people. So … it's not wrong to talk about how much you give, as long as it's to encourage others to give generously to God, not to promote your own benevolence. As a hedge against boasting, I encourage people if they feel led to share, to share percentages, not actual dollar amounts; to talk about lifestyle choices and sacrifice; and to humbly receive the joy of seeing their money have meaning in the kingdom.

A few years ago, I wanted to follow King David's example for myself and our board members who lead the church. I believe our team should be the leaders in the church and that God will honor their faith and obedience. I told them how much Becca and I were giving, and I asked them to give a certain amount to Kingdom Builders. They all jumped on board, and some gave more than I asked for. I also had conversations with our staff team. In a couple of cases, we talked in private. I challenged them as leaders and said, "If everyone in the church gave at the level you're giving, would we be able to do all that God has put on our hearts?"

Each one replied, in one way or another, "No, we wouldn't."

"So," I continued, "do you want to step out in faith and participate in plan-vision-dream?"

To create and keep momentum for giving, we extensively use videos throughout the year. People's minds can wander when they listen to music or the message, but videos more powerfully capture their attention, and the images of people in need and our work to care for them give them encouragement that their participation will make a huge difference. A video says, "Your giving made a big difference. See it here!"

Some critics look at our emphasis on generosity at River Valley and tell me, "You're way out of balance with raising money."

I reply, "I'm completely convinced we're doing what God has called us to do, so I'm unapologetic about asking people to give. God has given us a heart for people in our neighborhoods and around the world, and to be God's hands, feet, and voice to them, we need the resources. Since 80 percent of all the wealth among the world's believers is in the hands of American Christians, surely God wants us to be generous to support His desire for all to hear the Good News. We don't badger anybody to give. We just share the opportunity to make a difference and invite them to join us. Many do, some don't. God is at work, and He wants to expand His kingdom. It's our privilege to partner with Him. If we stop asking people to give to a cause much bigger than themselves, it'll show that we've lost our vision. I won't let that happen."

> **I'm completely convinced we're doing what God has called us to do, so I'm unapologetic about asking people to give.**

We're inviting people to join hands with God in a meaningful, joyful experience of seeing our resources used to change lives. We don't manipulate; we don't use guilt as a motivation, and we don't look down on people who aren't ready yet or say no to the offer. It's up to us to make the offer, and it's up to God to work in others' hearts to give them the desire to respond. We don't cross that line between our responsibility and His. We believe having a heart and a lifestyle of generosity is the very best way to live. After all, it's the example of Jesus, who gave himself "as a fragrant offering" to God out of His love for us (Ephesians 5:2).

If anyone should have been disqualified to lead the charge toward generosity, it's me. You read about all the mistakes at the beginning of the journey. How is it possible that God would use someone like me to raise tens of millions to spread the love of Christ around the world? Not long ago, Dave Ramsey and I had dinner together. We laughed and were awed by the fact that both of us had made incredibly dumb decisions about money early in our lives, but now God is using us to help people manage money so they're free from the crushing weight of debt and they give themselves and their resources to touch individuals, families, and organizations around the world. I'm amazed every time I think about it. I love what Dave says, "Outrageous generosity is the most fun you will ever have with money."

chapter nine

Maybe You

If you've read this far in the book, I have to believe God is tugging at your heart. He's giving you a vision of how He can use you in bigger ways and how your giving can touch more people. You may be ready to join the rest of us on this exciting journey … or you may already be on it, and you just love to read about others who are traveling alongside you. But you may have read this far and still have some questions, some doubts, and some resistance to the changes God may want you to make. I get it. I spend a lot of my time talking with people who have concerns and objections, so let me address some of them.

"I don't think I have enough faith to be generous."

It's not the size of your faith that matters; it's the power, love, and faithfulness of the One you believe in. I'd rather have a little faith in a big God than a lot of faith in a small God. Thankfully, our God is infinitely more loving, wise, kind, and powerful than anything we can imagine. All you need is enough faith to start with what you have now and do what you can.

"You're asking too much too soon. I'm not sure I'm ready for plan-vision-dream."

In my experience, the bottleneck of giving is in the commitment to tithe. When people are obedient to give ten percent, they make significant adjustments in their spending, and they begin to see God's blessings for their faithfulness. If you're not tithing, don't worry about plan-vision-dream. Ask God to give you the courage to begin giving ten percent and watch Him work in and through you in amazing ways. After this becomes a habit, most people embrace plan-vision-dream with great excitement!

"I want to give more, but my spouse isn't too thrilled about it."

Disagreements about money are seldom, if ever, standalone issues in a marriage. Other topics are inevitably friction points. A psychologist commented that the four reasons couples come to see him are different sexual preferences, strained relationships with in-laws, differing methods of raising their kids, and conflicts over money. Some researchers even point to money problems as the biggest reason for divorce! It's important that neither spouse strongarms the other into giving. It needs to be a mutual commitment and a shared dream. If several discussions and plenty of prayer don't get you to an agreement on giving, you should probably look at deeper, broader patterns of self-protective behaviors that are causing you to be distant from or antagonistic toward one another.

> I'd rather have a little faith in a big God than a lot of faith in a small God.

One suggestion for dual-income homes is for the spouse who wants to tithe and give to do it on his or her income only and see what God does in their life. This isn't meant to be a moment of shame each month but rather an opportunity to share the ways God moves through generosity. I thank God for the unity that Becca and I have, and I pray you and your spouse will find this same harmony.

"If I make a commitment and don't get there, I'll look foolish … and I'll feel terrible."

I've told a lot of glowing stories about people who had big goals, and God provided in miraculous (and sometimes very unexpected) ways, but there are others who come up short at the end of the year. Some have had unforeseen expenses, like high medical bills they hadn't anticipated, and others didn't see the provision they expected. I always tell people, "Good for you that you stepped out in faith! Way to go! Give it another shot next year and see what God does. Your giving this year wasn't a failure, and it wasn't because God turned His back on you. We don't understand all the mysteries of God, and His path sometimes has twists and turns that surprise us … and may disappoint us for a while. Don't give up on yourself or Him. Celebrate what you were able to do and the good that resulted because of your generosity."

"My giving won't even make a dent, so why even try?"

I hope by now you've put that fear to bed. The vast majority of people at River Valley give less than $1,000 over their tithe, and those are the ones working plan-vision-dream! The world isn't won for Christ because a few give generously; it's won because many give generously. Every dollar counts. Every dollar goes toward resources, services, or people who touch the lives of people in need. Your gift counts, no matter how big or how small. The church can't do this without you! God will be pleased with your faith and obedience.

"Plan-vision-dream feels risky."

Has there ever been an adventure without a measure of risk? (The answer is no.) Think of your favorite action movies. In each one, the hero faces uncertainty, unexpected detours and setbacks, and times when hope seems lost. But in our story, hope is never lost. We serve a God who delights in us taking calculated risks for His glory. Calculated? Yes. When we pray and ask Him for direction, He gives it. That's our assurance that we're on the right track. Will there be peril? Of course. Will we wonder if we'll make it? From time to time. But God is faithful. He'll see us through.

In my conversations with people, I've made two observations: First, some people, like Becca, are wired to be risk averse. That's not a flaw. Where in the world would I be without Becca's steady hand and cautious questions? But other people use risk as an excuse to sit on their hands (and wallets) and do nothing. If you're like Becca, hang out with people who encourage you to take a single bold step. If you're using risk as an excuse, ask God to give you a vision of how your giving can have a phenomenal impact on people.

"I value the security my money gives me."

To some extent and in different ways, all of us value security. Some seek it in the size of their bank accounts and retirement investments, and others look for it in job permanence, their spouse, the affirmation of friends, beauty, intelligence, or good health. It's certainly not wise to be insecure in too many areas of our lives, but far too often, as we've seen, money has us in its clutches, promising not only security but also pleasure, power, and popularity. And yes, it does buy those things ... in small measure for a short while, but we eventually end up feeling empty and foolish for trusting a commodity to give us what only God can provide.

The goal of life is not to die with the most money. If you are hoarding, I pray that you will get a revelation of how much good God can do with your generosity.

"I want to be able to provide for my family (or grandkids) in a way that makes them comfortable."

Providing for your family is the right thing to do, and after that, I challenge you to pursue adventure over comfort. Think about it, what brings out the best in people, focusing on things we can control or the adrenaline rush of attempting great things for God? Your family needs you, but they need your example of undaunted faith

> **The goal of life is not to die with the most money.**

far more than they need one more gadget or car or vacation. They need you to model what it looks like for your life to count and your money to have meaning, glad to sacrifice for the greatest cause in the universe.

Some of my greatest joys have been taking Connor and Logan with me on missions trips so they could participate in sharing the love of Jesus—in words, food, and labor—with people who desperately need what we can offer. Was it always comfortable? Definitely not. Was it life-changing? Just ask them.

"I have big plans for my retirement. I don't want to jeopardize that."

I don't want to be rude, but let me make an observation: I can't find retirement in the Scriptures. Before you get mad at me, let me explain! I see Abraham serving God into old age, Moses leading God's people well after being eligible for Medicare, Caleb marching his old body into the hill country during the conquest and saying, "Give me that mountain!" We may need to cut back on our efforts as we age, but if anything, our passion should grow as we see God work wonders. Our vision broadens as we see new opportunities to partner with God. We might retire from a particular career, but we never retire from loving, obeying, and serving God. Some of the most generous and energetic people I know would be considered "past their prime," but it appears they're in a new version of the prime of life. They take great joy that the money they are giving is going all over the world even if their bodies don't leave the neighborhood anymore!

> **We might retire from a particular career, but we never retire from loving, obeying, and serving God.**

"I'll leave a lot of money to the church in my will, but not now."

Some of the wealthiest people on the planet, like Bill Gates and Warren Buffett, have signed what they call "The Giving Pledge." The intent is to give at least half of their net worth away before they die or upon their death. T. Boone Pickens made a fortune in the oil business, and he gave away hundreds of millions. In an interview about his philanthropy, he explained, "I have a unique approach to giving. While many others of my status endow foundations that spin out millions of dollars over the course of generations, I want to see the good that's done with my money today while I'm alive and not wonder what is done with it long after I'm gone."[27] Or, to paraphrase him: I'm giving while I'm living, so I know where it's going.

I want to encourage you to do both! Give while you're living, and give in your final will and testament. Becca and I will be giving one last tithe and one last Kingdom Builders gift after we breathe our last breath!

Why do some people cling to their wealth? There may be many

reasons, but at least one of them is pure, old-fashioned greed. Jesus told people, "Watch out! Be on your guard against all kinds of greed; life does not consist in an abundance of possessions" (Luke 12:15 NIV). Commentators have pointed out that Jesus never said, "Watch out! You might commit adultery!" because we *aren't* surprised to hear about yet another couple trying to recover from the pain caused by an unfaithful spouse. Those instances are far too common, and they keep us aware of the dangers of adultery. But greed is far more insidious. One pastor did a series on "the seven deadly sins." His wife told him, "You'll have plenty of people who come to hear about adultery and gluttony, but they'll stay away in droves when you talk about greed." She was right. Nobody thinks they have a problem with greed. Why? Because we can always point to someone who has more money than we do, so we feel inferior to them. If we feel inferior, we conclude that we must not be greedy.

It's interesting that right after Jesus told us, "Store your treasures in heaven," He launched into a topic that seemed unconnected, and then He went back to talk about money: "You cannot serve God and be enslaved to money." What's the part in the middle? He said, "Your eye is like a lamp that provides light for your body. When your eye is healthy, your whole body is filled with light. But when your eye is unhealthy, your whole body is filled with darkness. And if the light you think you have is actually darkness, how deep that darkness is!" (Matthew 6:22-23). What's that about? I believe it's clearly connecting both of the concepts about money, and here, Jesus is telling us that it's very easy to be blind to the inordinate desire for money and the impact of that hyper-desire. When we're blinded by our longing for more money, we live in darkness, and if we think we're really sharp about how we manage our money, it only shows that we're deep into the darkness!

So, watch out! Open your eyes. Be on guard against *any form* of greed: for money, power, pleasure, possessions, and popularity. If you set your heart's affections on the wrong things, they'll eat you alive from the inside out.

You might need to work through one or more of these objections, or you may have others. Be sure to devote enough time to each potential roadblock because I'm inviting you to join all of us who are already on the journey of generosity. Ask all the questions you want to ask, but sooner or later, take the first step.

Let me tell you about some people who said, "Yes, it's me! I'm all in." These people are more than happy to share the joy of giving generously.

My mother has been a widow for two decades, but nothing slows her down. She's a Kingdom Builder, and she has enormous joy in giving to projects and people that touch her heart. She's on a fixed income, but every time she gives, she tells me, "I love that I get to build God's kingdom!" (When she learned what could be accomplished with $1,200, she was overjoyed that she could help so much on a fixed income!)

Lukas's life looked successful to most people, but he secretly was suffering a living hell from alcoholism. He wanted to feel alive and fulfilled, but he felt numb and empty. He remembers, "I knew that if I kept drinking, I'd never be the dad I wanted to be. There's no way living a lie was going to produce good fruit with my children." When he and his wife came to River Valley Church, they sensed something different. There, he found out about the Minnesota Adult and Teen Challenge faith-based treatment program. He knew he needed to go there, but he was scared. "What would life be like without my addiction? What will people say about me if I go to treatment? What stigma is attached to that? I could name a dozen reasons not to go."

After a couple of years of attending River Valley, his wife, Denise, decided to go on a mission trip to Ethiopia. While she was away, Lukas hit his "absolute rock bottom." He recalls, "It's the first time I felt genuine godly sorrow. My wife was halfway around the world, pregnant with our second child, and I was at home as a complete disaster. I knew it was now or never."

When his wife returned, Lukas announced, "I'm going into treatment."

Two weeks later, when he met with a nurse for intake, she told him, "Normally, I wouldn't admit you until you go through medical detox, but I can see it in your eyes that you're ready, so I'm going to admit you now."

After a week of no contact with anyone outside the treatment center, Denise and Lukas's son came for a visit. His son ran to him with his arms outstretched, and his wife was filled with joy that he was finally getting the help he needed. In that moment, Lukas thought, "*I'm never going back to the way things were!*" And he prayed, "God, whatever You have to do in me, I'm ready." That was the moment every-thing changed.

After he got out of treatment, Lukas left his job and started his own sign-making company so he could spend more time with his boys. He reflected, "I've never heard anyone say, 'I spent too much time with my dad.'"

Instead of alcohol sucking the life out of Lukas, he has become a giver—to his wife and sons, and his family have become generous Kingdom Builders. A few years before, no one would have imagined the transformation God produced in him.

———

Brad and Michelle are a couple in our church who have enjoyed successful careers. Each Janu-ary, they set aside time to pray and ask, "We want to do as much as we can. God, what do You want to do through us this year?" They set aside money for other projects beyond their Kingdom Builders vision. Now, when they talk to someone who is going on a mission trip and is raising money, they can say, "Send us a letter to let us know how much you need." Brad reflects, "It's really fun to get organized and have a plan and then see where God takes it."

One year, as the Kingdom Builders banquet approached, Brad received a much larger bonus than he expected. He and Michelle had already set their vision goal, but now they began praying to see how God might use the additional money they'd received. They sat across from each other at their dining room table as they prayed, and they each wrote a number on a napkin. They swapped napkins, and they instantly realized they'd written the same number. Michelle explains, "It's so fun to give. It's so fun to be generous."

"We want to be as generous as possible," Brad says. "Some years, the amount will be more than others, but we'll always do what we can to be generous. Planning at the beginning of the year makes it more fun. At first, Michelle wasn't too excited about making the plan, but when she saw how much we were able to give, she said, 'Give me that calculator! I want to see how much we can give!' It's exciting. We look forward to being generous."

We even teach the principles in this book to inmates through our prison ministry. The prisoners tithe on what they earn from jobs at the prison, and some of them send money over the tithe to Kingdom Builders. One offering we got was $1.20. It may not seem like much to most, but it's a sure sign of a heart touched by God. The note with it said, "I want you to know that I'm in. I want to help change the world for Jesus." Remember, it's not the amount, it's the obedience. (And in this case, it was a sacrificial gift that will catch the attention of Heaven and make a difference!)

One of the local projects that excites people is kids' camp. Every summer, our church helps fund kids and teens going to Lake Geneva Camp in Alexandria, Minnesota. Emily has been a counselor at camp for years, and as her three daughters grew up, they transitioned from campers to counselors. She talks about the impact: "I love kids' camp. The kids love it, and we get to build relationships with them over the days we're together. It's a great mix of fun during the day and meaningful times at chapel every night. The first time I was a counselor, two of my girls were there as campers. On the first night, I stood at the back of the chapel, watching God at work in the lives of 800 kids, and my eyes filled with tears. As a parent, it was so meaningful to know my daughters were involved. It was a defining moment for me, a time I'll never forget."

Emily reflected on the camp's long-term impact: "We value the next generation. I'll always give to see these kids raise their hands in full surrender to the Lord and later become leaders. I would tell anybody that their gift is multiplied in the Kingdom of God. That's God's math. That's how we see a kingdom impact."

When Josh was a young man, he prepared himself to take advantage of opportunities in real estate. He and his wife, Kelsie, joined River Valley, and we invited them to our banquet. There, they heard about plan-vision-dream, and they made a commitment to fund a translation of the Scriptures to provide Bibles for people who didn't have one in their own language. Josh explains, "Kelsie and I went to the banquet with a clear plan of what we wanted to give, but when we heard about the need, the Holy Spirit prompted us to add a zero to that number. The only way to hit that number was to sell our first piece of property, which we agreed to do and started down that path. But God had other plans. We were offered an early buyout opportunity of a license agreement, which provided the money for our Kingdom Builders gift … and even more. That was the first time I gave gladly instead of out of obligation, stretching to let God direct my giving. My own dream was to build a portfolio of real estate, so selling property was a real commitment. He was asking, 'Are you willing to give up your dreams for Me?' I learned that we can lean into the Lord, and He'll catch us every time."

The next January, Josh and Kelsie prayed about their Kingdom Builders gift for that year. When the Lord impressed Josh with a number, he did a double take. He asked Kelsie if the Lord had given her a number, and she responded, "The Lord doesn't speak to me in numbers. If He gave you one, let's give it!" She remembers concluding, "The Lord's plans are always greater. We don't get to be part of them if we don't say yes." During the year, God provided in incremental ways. By the fall, Josh and Kelsie were confident that God would come through so they could give their dream goal.

A wealthy man in our church planned to buy a red Ferrari. It was his dream car. (I know the feeling. I've had plenty of daydreams of driving a Porsche 911!) While he was wrestling with the decision, I spoke one Sunday about radical generosity, and I said, "You don't need a red Ferrari. Use that money to change lives."

After the service, he texted me, "Pastor Rob, did you have a word from God about me?"

I had no idea what he was talking about, so I replied, "What do you mean?"

He said, "I was thinking about buying a red Ferrari, but I want to live with different priorities. Thanks for calling me out this morning."

I was just using a random illustration, it might have been inspired, who knows! But now there's one less red Ferrari in Minnesota and a lot more orphanages and churches being built all over the world.

———

Someone in our church owns a large construction company, which has been very successful. As he was exposed to the mission of reaching the lost and caring for the least, his heart was touched. When he started his company, I'm sure his primary motivation was to be financially successful—nothing wrong with that—but now his motivation is to send more missionaries into the field to spread the Good News around the world. He has been on a number of global teams (the term our church uses for missions trips), so he's gotten to see how his gifts are making a huge impact. Now, he's one of the greatest encouragers to business owners to think beyond the here and now and live instead to hear God say, "Well done."

The stories are almost endless. If any of these people were asked, "Do you want to be a Kingdom Builder and use everything you are and everything you have to build Christ's kingdom?" they wouldn't say, "Maybe." They've said, "Yes! Absolutely! I wouldn't miss this for the world." No one is too far in debt; no one is too rich; no one is too young, and no one is too old. If an alcoholic, a successful couple, prisoners, and a wealthy business owner can be moved by the mission, you can too.

Imagine an Air Force pilot whose bomber is loaded with a "bunker buster," the most powerful non-nuclear bomb ever made. Our allies are in trouble, and they desperately need this pilot to help them, but he's preoccupied with polishing the wings on his multi-million dollar plane and detailing the tires. But then imagine a pilot who listens to the cries of those in trouble and flies into a barrage of flak to deliver the bomb and save his friends.

We need to ask, "Why did God create me to live during the wealthiest time in human history? Why did He put me here now, with all the technological and communication advances that make it far easier to reach people in remote areas of the globe? Why me? Why here? Why now?"

The better question is, "Why *not* me? Why *not* here? Why *not* now?"

This is the humility and gratitude King David had after God reminded him that he had been an afterthought when Samuel came to his family to anoint a new king. But God used a boy who wasn't even valued by his parents and brothers to rescue Israel from the Philistines and establish a kingdom in Israel. David was overwhelmed that God would use someone like him to accomplish something so magnificent, so he prayed,

> "Who am I, O Sovereign LORD, and what is my family, that you have brought me this far? And now, Sovereign LORD, in addition to everything else, you speak of giving your servant a lasting dynasty! Do you deal with everyone this way, O Sovereign LORD?
>
> "What more can I say to you? You know what your servant is really like, Sovereign LORD. Because of your promise and according to your will, you have done all these great things and have made them known to your servant...
>
> For you are God, O Sovereign LORD. Your words are truth, and you have promised these good things to your servant. And now, may it please you to bless the house of your servant, so that it may continue forever before you. For you have spoken, and when you grant a blessing to your servant, O Sovereign LORD, it is an eternal blessing!" (2 Samuel 7:18-21, 28-29)

No arrogance. No comparison. David was blown away by God's sweeping generosity to him, so he responded with genuine humility and a renewed passion to please the One who had proven so devoted to him. David looked forward to the fulfillment of a dynasty for Israel.

And those who have said yes to the call of generosity have prayed prayers like David's. We look forward to the rule and reign of the Lord Jesus over every tribe, tongue, and nation—at least partially now but completely when He returns. That's our true calling. That's His promise.

Are you in?

chapter ten

Living the Life

I've already mentioned Randy Alcorn's book, *The Treasure Principle*, which is one of the most significant books about God's perspective on how we should manage the resources God puts in our hands. He pans back to describe the wider picture of what's really important:

> I think of our lives in terms of a dot and a line, signifying two phases. Our present life on Earth is the dot. It begins. It ends. It's brief. However, from the dot, a line extends that goes on forever. That line is eternity, which Christians will spend in Heaven. Right now, we're living *in* the dot. But what are we living *for?* The shortsighted person lives for the dot. The person with perspective lives for the line.[28]

This was an eye opener to me, and I have to admit, almost every purchase Becca and I make is through the lens of the dot and the line. The only way we have even been able to make certain purchases is to set a budget so we know that so much more is going to the line and not the dot. I remember once that a friend challenged us early in our marriage to make sure we give more to the work of the Lord than we would even spend on our mortgage. At the time, I thought it was impossible. But now with God's grace, we are giving more to the Lord than any other expenditure in our life! When you're living for the line, there's a greater joy than I can explain; it's a supernatural peace and purpose that I wish everyone would experience.

Even though Becca and I are living for the line, there are moments that test you and really challenge you to live out what you believe. In December 2019, I was praying, and I sensed God say, "You're going to give your dream goal." (Remember Plan, Vision, Dream?) It was an amount Becca and I had been praying about for ten years, a figure we hoped we could give someday, but it would take an act of God. And He acted! In January, I told our church that the Lord was going to provide what we were praying for (because I felt that God wanted me to go public with the goal, but not the amount) and that Becca and I were going to give our dream goal to Kingdom Builders at the Miracle Offering in the fall.

At about the time I made that announcement, I read some sketchy reports of a virus that had been discovered in a city in China. No problem, right? Then some people in Seattle died from it, and soon, it spread to all parts of the globe. COVID-19 surprised us all as we thought nothing could stop our progress; oh, how we were wrong! It stopped us all in our tracks and shut down the world! All of us experienced lockdowns, mask mandates, supply chain problems, toilet paper shortages (remember that?), online work and church, and a stock market meltdown. Then, on May 25, George Floyd was killed here in Minneapolis, and protest marches were held across the country. Suddenly, the American economy didn't look like it was a favorable year to give a dream gift to our church or any charity. To be honest, if I hadn't declared it in a sermon that was *on video*, I may have just crossed this goal off my goal list for the year and figured I just missed God's voice.

Yet, as the year progressed, God provided for us in ways we didn't plan on or expect. Just before the Miracle Offering in November, the entire amount of money for our dream goal was sitting in our bank account, the largest amount we would ever give to the Lord but I looked at Becca and said, "Maybe we should hold on to this, just in case. The economy is uncertain; COVID is still killing people; we have a new president, and we have no idea what's going to happen in the coming year. All of this could really get out of hand."

My mind began playing tricks on me. I told Becca, "I don't know, maybe we should hold on to the money just in case." She agreed, and we decided to sleep on it. So we went to bed with "just in case" rolling around in our dreams.

Except neither of us got a wink of sleep all night. By morning, both of us had come to the conclusion after tossing and turning that we needed to write the check and give the entire amount at the Miracle Offering. We determined not to believe the lie of "just in case." God is our source, and He provided. If things got tough, we were confident He would provide again. It wasn't time to be afraid, listen to a lie, and back away. So we decided to give it, and the peace of God flooded our lives that very moment.

That weekend, I told the church about believing the lie of "just in case" and how the Lord had assured us that we needed to follow through by trusting Him even in an uncertain future. I told them that Becca and

We determined not to believe the lie of "just in case." God is our source, and He provided.

I decided to be obedient with the dream gift. It seems that other people had been wrestling with the same lie because the floodgates opened, and over the next few weeks, people gave an enormous amount of money. In fact, over $4 million was given in a 40-day window! Only God could make that happen!

The enemy might use an entire arsenal of lies for different people, but "just in case" was the lie that tied Becca and me in knots of fear, if only for a night. But once we broke its hold over us, so did our entire church.

As Becca and I struggled with the enemy's lie, we were tempted to live for the dot, and specifically, in fear that the dot would be a smudge! We chose to live for the line and have never regretted it.

In order to fight the lies that our giving doesn't make a difference or that we should live for the dot and not the line, we make a big push to ask people to go on missions trips. Those who go are on a wide spectrum of motivation: Some are just trying to find out what being a Kingdom Builder is all about, and they want to see the projects and people for themselves; others are already committed to giving to these projects, and personal involvement is important to them; and others go because they've gone before, and now they're taking people with them. They're paying the vision forward to friends and family members who might be captured by what God is doing in those lands. As I've mentioned, those who go on these trips give seven times more when they come back. It's that life-changing after they see the good their generosity is doing. They also see first-hand a world that needs to know about the love of Jesus.

Matthew tells us that even for Jesus, seeing had an impact: "When he saw the crowds, he had compassion on them because they were confused and helpless, like sheep without a shepherd. He said to his disciples, 'The harvest is great, but the workers are few. So pray to the Lord who is in charge of the harvest; ask him to send more workers into his fields'" (Matthew 9:36-38). Someone might be hesitant to go on a missions trip, but something happens when the person sees the need and the multitudes. There's something powerful about *seeing* needs instead of just reading or hearing about them. Seeing touches our hearts far more. Seeing helps us overcome the lies and really live out what we believe.

Many years ago, B. B. Warfield studied the emotions of Jesus described in the Gospels. He found that one emotion was mentioned more than all the others combined: compassion. It means "to be moved to the depths in our love, empathy, and care for another person." In many situations in the four Gospels, Jesus stopped what He was doing to give focused attention to the person in front of Him. No one has ever had a more demanding job description, but in scene after scene, Jesus was moved so deeply that He stopped to show how much He cared.[29]

Another tool we've used to help people really live out the life of being generous is to show them that their giving made a difference. I'm not sure where I heard this, but I was told that when someone makes a gift to a charity or cause, they ask two questions. First, "did they get my gift?" And secondly, "Did it make a difference?" This is where our use of videos comes in, to answer the second question. Most people deal with numbers, quotas, to-do lists and rarely get to see changed lives. So it is important to show them that their giving has changed lives, and that's what these videos do.

When you are watching a video of children laughing and eating because you gave, your world gets larger, your heart expands, and you are living out your values. When you see a church that is full of people praising God that was built by your generosity, you can't help but be filled with joy because your giving made a difference. When you see water flowing out of a clean water well that you helped finance, you are overwhelmed with gratitude that you get to live, "Blessed to be a Blessing." Videos of completed projects are such a powerful tool to help us live generous lives.

I've noticed a path that most generous people follow, almost always without even noticing. They begin with "I plan." They consider what the Scriptures say about treasures, and they want their lives to count for more than the things they can stuff in their closets, garages, and stock portfolios. They begin to formulate a plan to use their money for the kingdom. As they take the first steps and see the impact of their giving, they gain confidence and believe, "I can. I can do this, and it really matters!" They realize God isn't using superstars; He uses regular people to do amazing things. After a while, giving becomes woven into the fabric of their lives. It's no longer as much of an effort; it's how they think, what they believe, and who they are. They start seeing the difference in real time. They realize, "I am a generous person. That's me. I plan … I can … I am."

As I've shared the process of plan-vision-dream, I've been incredibly encouraged by the response of pastors, church leaders, and their people. It's actually so simple: We listen to the Lord and do what He tells us to do. We pay attention to His whispers and nudges, and we make a plan to give an amount above our tithe. We ask God for a vision goal that stretches us a little or a lot more, and we trust Him to put a dream goal on our hearts that is far beyond anything we can do on our own. Is this challenging? You bet! Is it the way God wants us to live? I believe with all my heart that it is. But as I've written, it's not really about the money. Our intentional listening, our obedience, and our generosity to give even more is one of the ways we connect with the heart of God, and nothing is better than that!

My friend Mike Burnette uses a powerful illustration to show that living the life of generosity is the only one worth living: Imagine sitting at your favorite restaurant with some guests. In one chair sits an older lady who has been a missionary in a country where being a Christian is illegal. She lost her husband to cancer, but she stayed on the mission field because God has given her a deep love for the people in her city. She tells stories of God giving people dreams and visions of Jesus inviting them to come to Him, and the look on her face is one of sheer joy. She says, "My husband and I saw few people come to

Is this challenging? You bet! Is it the way God wants us to live? I believe with all my heart that it is.

Christ for many years, then there were a few drops, then a trickle, and now there's a stream. I've begun to dream that God might cause a mighty river of people who respond to the love of Jesus."

The person sitting across from you is a missionary in another part of the world. He shares the heartbreaking story of a young man he led to Christ who was killed by neighbors because of his new faith. He says his own life has been threatened, but he insists, "I'm going to stay and tell people about Jesus because He's their only hope now and for eternity."

In the other chair is a young man who is a relatively new believer. He lives in a city in Tanzania where Kingdom Builders invested to build a church that seats 5,000 people. To prove he's a man to the elders of his tribe, he has to murder someone from a rival tribe. That's his initiation into adulthood. But before he kills, someone in the church shares the gospel with him; he trusts in Jesus, and he goes to the rival tribe, not to murder but to minister the grace of God to anyone who will listen.

At the end of the meal and the incredible conversations, the waiter brings the check. What do you do? You practically jump out of your chair to grab that check and insist, "I'm paying for this!" You turn to the lady and tell her, "It's the least I can do to appreciate your love and sacrifice for the people whom you serve!" You turn to the missionary whose disciple was killed and who has been threatened with death, and you say, "It's the least I can do for someone who is giving his all to Christ and His cause!" You then turn to the young man whose life's trajectory was radically refocused by the love of God and say, "It's the least I can do for someone who has experienced and is expressing grace so powerfully!"

Each of these stories represent real people we support through our giving. Each one is in the trenches every day, suffering ridicule and risking much worse. And that's our response when we become aware of the overflowing love of God's people, who are pouring themselves out into the lives of those who have never heard the Gospel and don't know the love they can enjoy in a relationship with Christ.

That's the attitude I want you to have when you hear the principles of plan-vision-dream. I want you to be so excited about playing a part in the effective ministries of missionaries, agencies, and organizations around the corner and around the world that their hearts are moved to dig deeper and give more, not because you have to but because you can't imagine living

> **I just want people to pray, listen to God's voice, and follow His lead. When we do this, God adds meaning to our money and we live generous lives that change the world.**

any other way. Most of us wish we could give much more, but we give all we can because "it's the least I can do." Our heart's desire isn't to keep as much as possible, to spend on ourselves as much as we can, but to use everything God entrusts to us to maximize the reach of the kingdom into lives near and far. We want to continue to give more and keep growing in our generosity.

Are you feeling God's prompting? I've talked with people who heard God's whispered invitation to give more, and they wonder if it's really God's nudge. I ask them, "Who else would it be? Does anyone else care as much about the vulnerable and setting captives free?" I don't want anyone to try to talk themselves into generous giving or feel pressured in any way. I just want people to pray, listen to God's voice, and follow His lead. When we do this, God adds meaning to our money and we live generous lives that change the world. More than the good we do around the world, the good God does in our lives is even more substantial. It enlarges our heart; it breaks the gravitational pull of "stuff" and helps us reflect the heart of God, who gave first.

When we live this out, and we live blessed to be a blessing, it results in God being praised and a joy in our lives that nothing on this earth can match. My prayer for you is that you live a generous life, with meaning to your money and your eyes focused on the "Well done" that is waiting for you when you leave this world behind!

Endnotes

1 | This story is also found at the beginning of Chapter 7 in *Fix It!*

2 | Charles Spurgeon, "The Overflowing Cup," Metropolitan Tabernacle Pulpit Volume 21, January 1, 1970, https://www.spurgeon.org/resource-library/sermons/the-overflowing-cup-2/#flipbook/

3 | Charles Haddon Spurgeon, A sermon preached on August 27, 1868, https://www.spurgeon.org/resource-library/sermons/a-cheerful-giver-beloved-of-god/

4 | *Rabbi Hayim Halevy Donin, To Be A Jew. (New York: Basic Books, 1972). p. 48.*

5 | "About the Righteous," Vad Vashem, https://www.yadvashem.org/righteous/about-the-righteous.html

6 | J. Matthew Wilson, *From Pews to Polling Places: Faith and Politics in the American Religious Mosaic (Georgetown University Press, 2007), pp. 140-142.*

7 | Rodney Starks, *The Rise of Christianity* (Princeton: Princeton University Press, 2006), p. 161.

8 | Randy Alcorn, *The Treasure Principle* (New York: Multnomah, 2017), p. 100.

9 | "Bible Verses about Money and Stewardship," https://www.envoyfinancial.com/participantresources/bible-verses-about-money-and-stewardship

10 | Viviana A. Zelizer, Ph.D., "When We Were Socially Distant, Money Brought Us Closer," *New York Times*, February 19, 2022, https://www.nytimes.com/2022/02/19/opinion/pandemic-charity-remittance.html

11 | "Where Do We Go from Here," Sharpe Group, November 2008, https://sharpenet.com/give-take/go/?highlight=great%20depression

12 | Taylor Schulte, "Charitable Giving Statistics for 2023," Define Financial, February 10, 2023, https://www.definefinancial.com/blog/charitable-giving-statistics/

13 | "What Is a Tithe? New Data on Perceptions of the 10 Percent," Barna, September 7, 2022, https://www.barna.com/research/what-is-a-tithe/

14 | Both quotes cited in *Beating the Odds*, iUniverse, 2009, p. 86.

15 | *William Barclay's Daily Study Bible*, "The Meaning of a Miracle (John 6:1-13), https://www.studylight.org/commentaries/eng/dsb/john-6.html

16 | Cited in *One Heart Full of Love*, edited by Jose Luis

Gonzalez Balado, https://jameslau88.com/2020/05/20/
love-until-it-hurts-by-mother-teresa-edited-by-jose-luis-gonzalez-balado/

17 | Global Commission Partners, https://www.globalcp.org/start-here

18 | Bible Study Tools, Easton's Bible Dictionary, Mammon, https://www.biblestudytools.com/dictionary/mammon/

19 | Thomas Chalmers, "The Expulsive Power of a New Affection," https://www.christianity.com/christian-life/spiritual-growth/the-expulsive-power-of-a-new-affection-11627257.html

20 | Jack Johnson, Anthony Cornelius Hamilton, & Mark Christopher Batson, "The News," © 2000 Songs of Universal Inc., Bat Future Music, Tappy Whyte's Music, Bubble Toes Publishing

21 | American Debt Statistics, https://shiftprocessing.com/american-debt/

22 | Adapted from "11 Questions to Ask Ourselves about Debt," Randy Alcorn, Eternal Perspective Ministries, https://www.epm.org/blog/2016/Jan/27/questions-debt

23 | "Hobby Lobby founder & CEO: Invisible qualities, not money, make life worth living," Fox News, April 25, 2017, https://www.foxnews.com/opinion/hobby-lobby-founder-ceo-invisible-qualities-not-money-make-life-worth-living

24 | Randy Alcorn, "Is It True You Advise Not Leaving Any Inheritance to Our Children," Eternal Perspective Ministries, March 10, 2017, https://www.epm.org/resources/2017/Mar/10/leave-inheritance-children/

25 | Zach Sharf, "Nicolas Cage Paid Off Debts with VOD Films, but He Stands by Every Role: 'I Never Phoned It In,'" *Variety*, March 22, 2022, https://variety.com/2022/film/news/nicolas-cage-defends-vod-films-debt-1235211377/

26 | "Here's How Many Millionaires and Billionaires Live in the United States," *Motley Fool*, March 15, 2023, https://www.fool.com/the-ascent/personal-finance/articles/us-millionaires-and-billionaires-you-might-not-believe-the-wealth/

27 | Marshall Scott, "T. Boone Pickens' History of Generous Giving at Oklahoma State," Pistols Firing, https://pistolsfiringblog.com/t-boone-pickens-history-of-generous-giving-at-oklahoma-state/

28 | "Live for the Line, Not the Dot," Randy Alcorn, December 17, 2014, https://www.epm.org/blog/2014/Dec/17/live-line

29 | B. B. Warfield, "The Emotional Life of Our Lord," www.deeperstudy.com/link/emotional_ebook_sample.pdf

Using Plan-Vision-Dream in Classes and Groups

This book is designed for individual study, small groups, and classes. The best way to absorb and apply these principles is for each person to study and answer the questions at the end of each chapter individually and then discuss them in either a class or a group environment.

Each chapter's questions are designed to promote reflection, application, and discussion. Order enough copies of the book for everyone to have a copy. For couples, encourage both to have their own book so they can record their individual reflections.

A recommended schedule for a small group or class might be:

Week 1
Introduce the material. As a group leader, tell your story of steps of generosity, share your hopes for the group, and provide books for each person. Encourage people to read the assigned chapter each week and answer the questions.

Weeks 2–11

Each week, introduce the topic for the week and share a story of how God has used the principles in your life. In small groups, lead people through a discussion of the questions at the end of the chapter. In classes, teach the principles in each chapter, use personal illustrations, and invite discussion.

Personalize Each Lesson

Don't feel pressured to cover every question in your group discussions. Pick out three or four that had the biggest impact on you and focus on those, or ask people in the group to share their responses to the questions that meant the most to them that week.

Make sure you personalize the principles and applications. At least once in each group meeting, add your own story to illustrate a particular point.

Make the Scriptures come alive. Far too often, we read the Bible like it's a phone book, with little or no emotion. Paint a vivid picture for people. Provide insights about the context of people's encounters with God and help people in your class or group sense the emotions of specific people in each scene.

Focus on Application

The questions at the end of each chapter and your encouragement to group members to be authentic will help your group take big steps to apply the principles they're learning. Share how you are applying the principles in particular chapters each week, and encourage them to take steps of growth, too.

Three Types of Questions

If you have led groups for a few years, you already understand the importance of using open questions to stimulate discussion. Three types of questions are *limiting, leading,* and *open*. Many of the questions at the end of each chapter's lesson are open questions.

Limiting questions focus on an obvious answer, such as, "What does Jesus call himself in John 10:11?" These don't stimulate reflection or discussion. If you want to use questions like this, follow them with thought-provoking, open questions.

Leading questions require the listener to guess what the leader has in mind, such as, "Why did Jesus use the metaphor of a shepherd in John 10?" (He was probably alluding to a passage in Ezekiel, but many people don't know that.) The teacher who asks a leading question has a definite answer in mind. Instead of asking this kind of question, you should just teach the point and perhaps ask an open question about the point you have made.

Open questions usually don't have right or wrong answers. They stimulate thinking, and they are far less threatening because the person answering doesn't risk ridicule for being wrong. These questions often begin with "Why do you think …?" or "What are some reasons that …?" or "How would you have felt in that situation?"

Preparation

As you prepare to teach this material in a group or class, consider these steps:

1. Carefully and thoughtfully read the book. Make notes, highlight key sections, quotes, or stories, and complete the reflection

section at the end of each day's chapter. This will familiarize you with the entire scope of the content.

2. As you prepare for each week's class or group, read the corresponding chapter again and make additional notes.

3. Tailor the amount of content to the time allotted. You won't have time to cover all the questions, so pick the ones that are most pertinent.

4. Add your own stories to personalize the message and add impact.

5. Before and during your preparation, ask God to give you wisdom, clarity, and power. Trust Him to use your group to change people's lives.

6. Most people will get far more out of the group if they read the chapter and complete the reflection each week. Order books before the group or class begins or after the first week.

Discussion Questions

chapter one

1. Are you more like me, a go-for-broke risk-taker, or more like Becca, more cautious about money? What are the upsides and downsides of your personality?

2. Do you know someone with a story of God coming through financially for them? How does the story affect you?

3. Do you agree or disagree with the idea that generosity "isn't really about money"? Explain your answer.

4. Think of as many ways as possible that God is generous to you, including the age you live in, your advantages of education, your most important relationships, and your talents and skills.

5. What do you hope to get out of this book?

chapter two

1. What's wrong with believing there's a finite pie of God's resources?

2. Read Job 38:2-7 (and read all of God's announcements to Job if you have time). What was God's message to him? How does that apply to your view of resources?

3. Who do you know who lives by the principle of "blessed to be a blessing"? What's that person's impact on you and others?

4. On a scale of 0 (not at all) to 10 (to the max), what's your normal level of gratitude? Explain your answer. What would it take for you to develop "a glass half-full with free refills" perspective?

5. What are three (or two or just one) specific people, organizations, or causes you could get excited about helping with your time, talents, or treasure? What difference would your involvement make to them and to you?

chapter three

1. Before reading this chapter, had you heard about the concept of tithing before? If so, what emotion was sparked by any mention of tithing? Where do you think that perspective came from?

2. Why is it helpful to realize that the tithe was first given hundreds of years before the Law was written?

3. Look back at the Old Testament passages in this chapter (specifically Leviticus 27:30, Deuteronomy 26:6-11, and Malachi 3:10-12). What do these passages say about the motivation to tithe?

4. What are some consequences of seeing the tithe as primarily transactional? What are the benefits of seeing it as relational?

5. Do you agree or disagree with the perspective that it's not biblical to suggest a gradual increase to the tithe? Explain your answer.

6. What do you think might happen if you believe the promise in 2 Corinthians 9:10-11?

7. What is God saying to you through this chapter?

chapter four

1. How do you think it changes individuals, couples, and churches to see a strategy like Kingdom Builders as a new way to live instead of a club for the wealthy?

2. What concepts, values, hopes, and fears about money did you absorb from your parents as a child? What specific memories about money from that time come to mind?

3. What are some ways you can teach and model generosity to your kids (or grandkids)? What impact do you hope you have on them regarding money?

4. Which excites you: providing buildings and resources for people on the other side of the world, caring for people in your city, or equipping rising leaders for the future? What about that cause captures your heart?

5. To think, pray, and live generously, we all have to make adjustments. What adjustments might you and your family need to make? What factors might be roadblocks or detours? What incentive will keep you going on the right path?

6. Where are you in your relationship with God? Are you still on the edge of the Grand Canyon, trying to jump as far as you can, or have you given up on your abilities and now trust only in Jesus to rescue you and make you a citizen of His kingdom?

7. If you trusted Christ to rescue you in the past, what are some reasons you need to keep trusting in His grace all day, every day? What difference will it (or does it) make?

chapter five

1. Is it inconceivable that you might want to give beyond what you are giving to support your local church? Why or why not?

2. What adjustments might you need to make if you craft a plan to give more than you do now? (If you've never done this, I want to encourage you to create a plan for giving and then work the plan.)

3. Take some time to ask God for a vision of how He might entrust some of what He has in His hands to you so you can give more to expand the kingdom. This will stretch you, but I believe God will give you a faith goal to pray for.

4. Ask God to put a dream in your heart, probably not yet a specific amount of money, but the beginning of an image of what God might want to do through you. As the dream becomes clearer, ask Him to give you a specific number as your dream goal. Then write it down in your private notebook!

5. Why is it important to realize God's kingdom is the opposite of the world—upside down, inside out, and backward forward?

6. Which of the stories at the end of the chapter encourages you the most? What about it touches your heart?

7. How would you explain the concept of plan-vision-dream to a friend?

chapter six

1. What are the parallels between building our giving muscles and building our actual muscles?

2. How do you think it would help the people in your church (and you) if your leaders had a regular monthly rhythm of asking, updating, celebrating, and resting?

3. What would it be like at your church if people gave so generously the pastor had to say, "Stop! You've given enough!"?

4. Where are you in the process of tithing, first planned gift, first vision goal, big steps up to five percent, and radical generosity of 20 percent or more? Where do you want to be? What difference would it make?

5. Review the statistics near the end of the chapter (about 80 percent of wealth in the hands of Christians is in America; 42 percent of the world has never heard a clear gospel presentation; and only one percent of missions giving is designated for unreached people groups). Do these numbers challenge you, discourage you, or inspire you? Explain your answer.

chapter seven

1. Why is it important to realize that "mammon" is more than a number . . . it's a god people worship? What are some signs that someone is worshiping mammon?

2. If a soul doctor did a checkup of your heart for God and the meaning of money, what would the doctor find regarding your daydreams, the stories you tell, what makes you cry, and what thrills you?

3. What's your accumulated blessing total as of today? Is it even important to you? Why or why not?

4. What were you thinking and feeling when you read the paragraphs about challenging people to give $1 million? What would motivate you to celebrate their generosity . . . instead of maybe being jealous or resentful that they have so much?

5. Take some time to celebrate in prayer the way God is using your generosity and the generosity of the people in your church.

6. What difference does it make to realize everything is going to burn?

7. So, what needs to change in your perspective and your giving to add meaning to your money?

chapter eight

1. Why is it important for churches to follow King David's pattern of giving first as an example to the leaders, then the other leaders become an example to everyone else, and then the rest of the people give joyfully and willingly?

2. How would you describe the "wave of generosity" we've created at River Valley? What are some practical ways you can apply these activities in your church?

3. If you're a parent or grandparent, how have you tried to instill a heart for generosity in your kids and grandkids? Do you think you've blown it through your words or actions? If you have, how can you rectify the mistake?

4. From the list of suggestions about encouraging kids to be generous, which ones will you use? What do you expect to happen?

5. Do you agree or disagree with my perspective that it's okay to tell people what you give as long as your motive is to inspire them instead of impressing them? Explain your answer.

chapter nine

1. What are some common excuses people use to avoid parting with more of their money through generous giving?

2. Which of those have you used? What's the antidote for each one?

3. Do you agree or disagree that to be on a mission with God, "No one is too far in debt, no one is too rich, no one is too young, and no one is too old"? What adjustments might each group need to make to be more generous?

4. Are you polishing your plane, or are you responding to the cries of your allies? Explain your answer.

5. Read David's prayer a couple of times, and then make it your own.

chapter ten

1. What are some ways a person can tell if he or she is living for the dot or the line? How about you?

2. How does the lie of "just in case" haunt us and keep us from trusting God?

3. What does "whole-life generosity" look like?

4. Give an example or two of people who live this way.

5. What kind of impact do they have on others? On you?

6. Are you living this way? Why or why not?

7. What does it say to you that Jesus' compassion is the emotion described more than any other in the Gospels?

8. Where are you in the process of "I plan," "I can," "I am"?

9. What does it mean to "stay in your lane"? How does it apply to you?

10. What's the most significant truth or concept you've gotten from reading this book? How are you applying it? What's your next step?

About the Author

As Lead Pastor of River Valley Church, Rob Ketterling is highly regarded for his vision and relentless passion to expand the Kingdom of God. He and his wife Becca planted River Valley in 1995, which has since grown to 11 locations in Minneapolis, Minnesota, and two international locations (Mbekelweni, eSwatini and Vancouver, Canada). Since founding River Valley, the church has given over $60 million to missions efforts around the world.

Rob has a down-to-earth preaching style, allowing his audience to take practical steps in their journey no matter where they are. He inspires people to live an authentic, faith-filled relationship with Jesus, and he challenges leaders at every level to change the world. Rob believes healthy churches should bring new people in, raise them up in their faith, and launch them in their God-given purpose. To date, River Valley has sent over 250 full-time missionaries, with a goal of sending 500.

Rob is a published author of seven books, including *Change Before You Have To*, *Front Row Leadership*, *Speed of Unity*, *Keep the Change*, and *The Generous Life*. He loves traveling, golf, and enjoying time with his wife Becca, their two sons Connor and Logan, his daughters-in-law Alexia and Mikayla, and his grandson Beckham.

Resources

CHANGE BEFORE YOU HAVE TO

What will it take for you to change? For most of us, it takes a crisis, a tragedy, a pain so great that change is actually forced upon us. By then, it's way too late. But what if you could find the strength to change before the pain, before the crisis, before the tragedy? No more excuses, no more good intentions, it's time to change and live life to the fullest!

THRILL SEQUENCE

Are you constantly looking for your next adrenaline-packed experience? Seeking another dose of excitement from an adventure with suspense, fun, and danger rolled into one? What if your Christian life were just as thrilling? Rob Ketterling encourages readers to seek adventure in a full-on, reignited faith. He challenges others to discover the excitement in passionately pursuing a life of service and reckless faith.

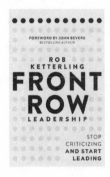

FRONT ROW LEADERSHIP

Become the person of influence you were born to be. Whether you're a CEO, a volunteer, or a home-maker, leadership is your responsibility. Rob Ketterling offers tools that will empower you to move up to the front and lead the change you want to see take place. Learn to engage the leadership process and contribute with your God-given strengths.

FIX IT!

Even before the smoke starts to rise, every leader sees the signals that something isn't right. Your wide variety of problems may vary in severity, scope, and timing, but they have one thing in common: people are looking to you to fix them all! But before you go running for the fire extinguisher, the duct tape, or to schedule an emergency meeting of your board of

elders, see what Pastor Rob Ketterling has to say. It may surprise you to discover that the problem isn't yours to fix.

SPEED OF UNITY

The Blue Angels and the Thunderbirds perform incredible feats of aero-nautics, but only because their minds, hearts, and bodies are perfectly synchronized. In the same way, leaders get the most out of their teams when they raise the level of unity. In this book, Rob's principles and advice will challenge you and inspire you to fight for a new speed, the Speed of Unity. This is only achieved when people are intentionally invested in the success of the team, not just individual accomplishments. Hang on. It's going to be a fast ride!

KEEP THE CHANGE

This is the sequel to Pastor Rob's earlier book, *Change Before You Have To*. It takes courage and tenacity to launch important changes, but far too often, distractions and difficulties slow our progress—and sometimes, our lives are thrown into reverse! With his usual wit and gift for telling stories, Pastor Rob, provides sound biblical principles, clear steps to take, and benchmarks to measure your progress. If you've ever wondered why it's so hard to make a change last, this book is for you!